101
Winning
Special Teams Drills

Michael A. Cieri

ISBN: 978-1-60679-143-1
Library of Congress Control Number: 2010918026
Cover design: Brenden Murphy
Book layout: Bean Creek Studio
Front cover photo: ©Frank Casimiro/ZUMA Press
Illustrations: Brenden Murphy

Coaches Choice
P.O. Box 1828
Monterey, CA 93942
www.coacheschoice.com

Dedication

To the memory of my parents—my dad, Anthony 'Chickie Boy' Cieri, and my mom, Caroline Cieri—who worked and sacrificed all their lives to give me the opportunities they never had. Their life together was one of caring and giving. And although they enjoyed all the good things of life—especially family and friends—they gave so much more than they took. It is hard to describe how much I miss them. I am comforted somewhat in knowing the multitude of lives they affected so positively.

To my best teammates in the world—my children, Carla Nicole Cieri, the physical therapist, and Michael Joseph Cieri, the very promising sports management graduate—who have been and always will be great sources of pride to me.

To Joyce Civello whose patience, understanding, and support make her an incredibly special person to me.

To the many coaches and players I have been privileged to work with over the years. They are the reason going to work every day has been so enjoyable.

Acknowledgments

To acknowledge all those who have passed on to me the knowledge presented in *101 Winning Special Teams Drills* and who have helped me formulate the ideas in this book would take a separate chapter. So, I will recognize a few specifically and others generally. I would like to thank the following:

The four head coaches who hired me over a 39-year span: Rick Giancola, Montclair State University; William Klika, Fairleigh Dickinson University; Jack Francis, Boonton High School, and Al Nicholas, Mount Olive High School. Each influenced me significantly and gave me the freedom to learn and thrive professionally.

The assistant football coaches—Rich O'Connor, Todd Agresta, Ron Gavazzi, Scott Santora, Josh Resto, Ron Cook, and Billy Walsh—and the student assistants—Scott Wisniewski, Nick Citro, and Jason Scott—who carried out the plan to make the special teams a priority.

The student-athletes who are the reason I am in this profession. I hope I've served you as well as you have energized my life. Thanks for the volumes you've taught me. Always remember that you can be a fierce competitor and "Do It Right."

Finally, the staff at Coaches Choice, especially Jim Peterson, for their professionalism in developing a quality product that would benefit players and coaches for years to come.

Contents

Preface

The heart of the special teams lies in the ability of the players to execute their techniques. The foundation of the special teams' sound and effective execution begins with the utilization of progressive drills that build the techniques required for making the schemes work. *101 Winning Special Teams Drills* provides special teams coordinators with effective methodologies and exercises to maximize the fundamentals of the special teams units.

This book sets forth how to make your special teams more proficient. The primary objective of the book is to thoroughly present drills that will develop the fundamentals necessary for effective special teams play regardless of the scheme. The drills and techniques will help to quickly build individual player skills and maximize practice time for your special teams.

The individual drills will ensure that the players understand the techniques, which is essential in the team concept. Team success will come from the improvement of individual player skills that will be obtained from these specific drills. The individual skill development drills can be performed in a circuit concept with stations, which will help increase the rate and degree of learning, thus improving your chances of winning the field position battle. Once individual skills are mastered, group drills can be used to build the coordination between players and the scheme. Team drills can then be utilized to simulate game-day situations. Finally, training routines for punters, kickers, snappers, returners, swatters, and stingers can be used to complete the compendium of drills that will help improve your special teams.

1

Skill Development
for Kickoff Coverage

#1: Split Double-Team (Individual)

Objective: To develop the technique for breaking up a double-team block from the kickoff return team

Equipment Needed: Shields

Description: Players align as shown in the diagram. The defender attacks the double-team block (shields) full speed. Using his hands, the defender shocks and locks the inside shoulder of one blocker, then sets his eyes to the other blocker as he continues to drive the initial blocker back. Then he dips his shoulder and rips through the double-team. He proceeds upfield once the double-team has been split and makes an angle tackle on the approaching ballcarrier.

Coaching Point: Make sure that the defender uses inside hand jams—not the shoulder pads—to break up the double-team.

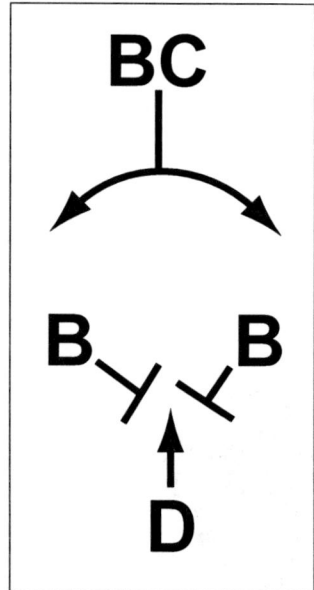

#2: Hardhat Fit (Individual)

Objective: To destroy the block at the point of attack

Equipment Needed: Shields

Description: The defender fits (locks up) with the blocker on a shield or with live players. On the go command, the defender and blocker drive their feet. The defender must push the blocker straight back, control the blocker, and escape with a rip technique as the ballcarrier approaches. He should make a form fit angle tackle.

Coaching Points:

- The defender must lock out the defender with both arms and use the feet before escaping to tackle the lead carrier.
- The blocker should attempt to turn the defender away from the ballcarrier's direction by swinging his hip between the defender and the ballcarrier.

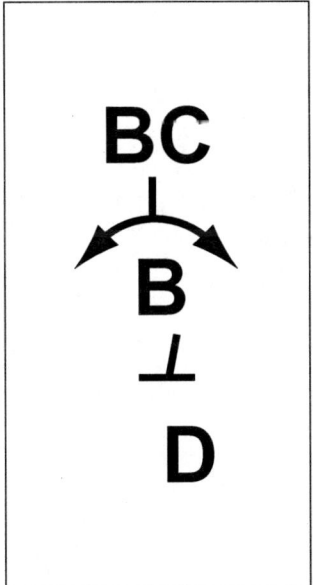

#3: Come to Balance (Individual)

Objective: To assure that the defender maintains body control when approaching the ballcarrier

Equipment Needed: Cones

Description: The defender approaches the ballcarrier at full speed from 15 yards away. When the defender is five yards in front of the cones, the ballcarrier runs straight upfield and angle runs to the left or right of the cone. The defender works on gathering his feet, cha-cha-ing forward, and making a proper angle tackle.

Coaching Point: The defender must continue to close in on the ballcarrier as the cones are approached, and never stop.

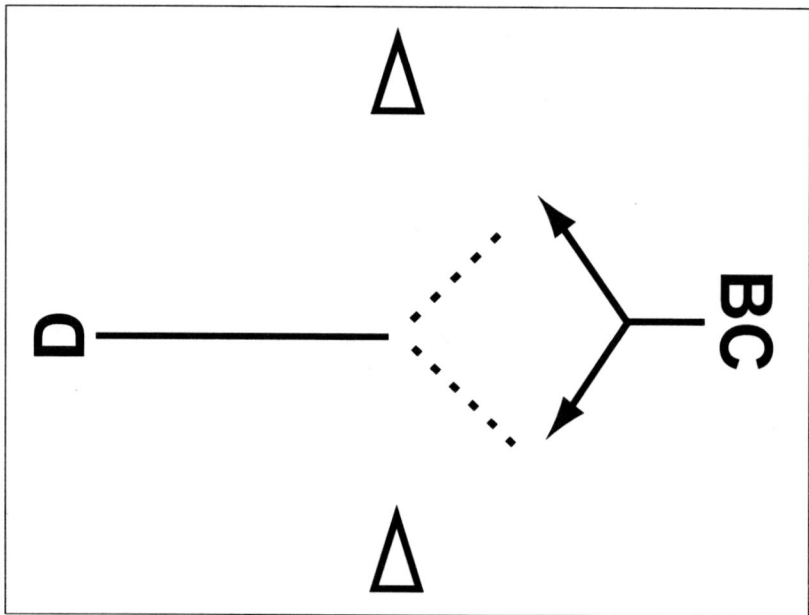

#4: Butt and Press (Individual)

Objective: To work on the proper technique of striking a blow on an angle block

Equipment Needed: Cones

Description: The defender takes off directly when the blocker starts the fishhook technique. The defender starts 8 to 10 yards from the blocker. When the defender engages the blocker, the defender jams his arms on the blocker, runs the feet, and drives the blocker back. When the blocker is driven back, the ballcarrier moves forward and angle runs left or right. The defender escapes with a rip or swipe technique and makes a proper angle tackle.

Coaching Points:

- The blocker must get to the fishhook spot and move toward the defender and then shock and lock with his hands on the defender.
- The defender must close on the blocker full speed.

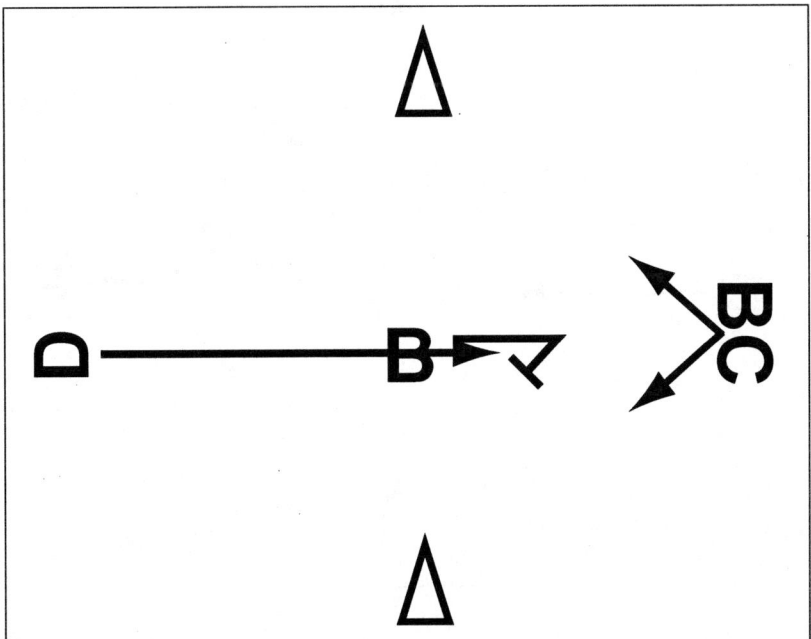

#5: Avoid Opposite—Reading the Upfield Shoulder (Individual)

Objective: To enhance the reading of the upfield shoulder of the front line on the kickoff return in order to maintain a proper coverage lane

Equipment Needed: Cones

Description: The defender starts down the field full speed. The blocker turns his shoulders (right or left). As the defender approaches the upfield shoulder of the blocker, the defender stems to the front numbers of the blocker, plants his outside foot, and crosses over the upfield shoulder. The defender proceeds to the ballcarrier, coming to balance and making a proper angle tackle.

Coaching Point: The defender must stay tight to the blocker after reading the upfield shoulder to maintain the proper coverage lane.

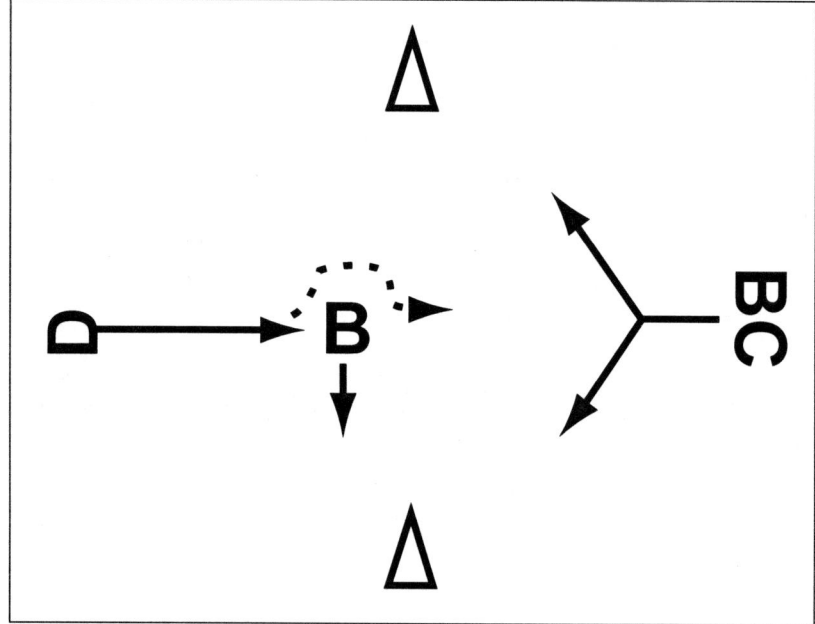

#6: Hard Turn—Improper Read of the Upfield Shoulder (Individual)

Objective: To teach the proper reaction after misreading the upfield shoulder and running past the leverage depth

Equipment Needed: Cones

Description: The defender runs downfield toward the blocker. As the defender approaches the blocker, the defender misreads the upfield shoulder and runs out of the lane around the blocker. The defender must plant on his outside foot and run the wheel. The defender needs to take a proper angle and form tackle the ballcarrier.

Coaching Points:

- The defender needs to stay tight to the blocker and rip under the blocker, making sure not to round off the pursuit angle.
- The defender should keep all movements sharp.

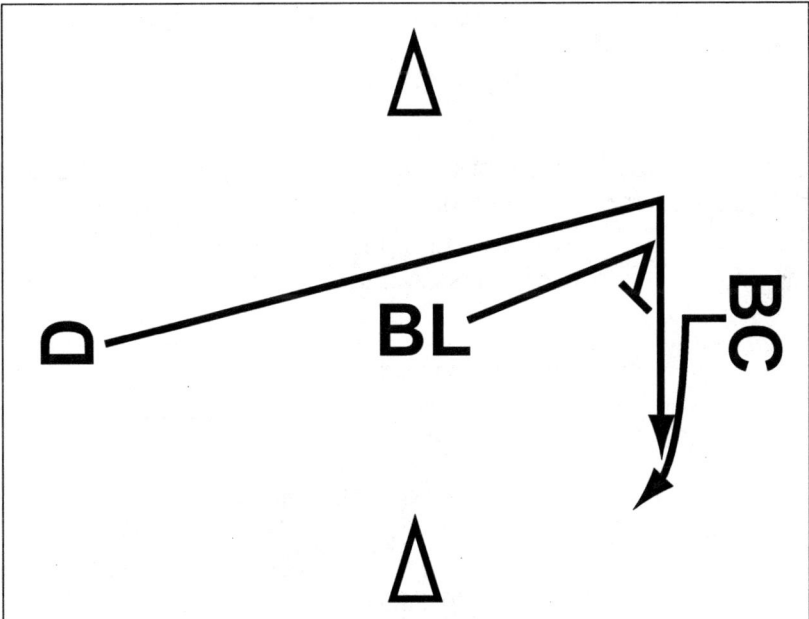

#7: Chaos (Individual)

Objective: To combine the various skills necessary to cover the kickoff with game-day simulation

Equipment Needed: Stand-up dummies, shields, agile bags, cones, stopwatch

Description: The drill is set up according to the diagram from sideline to sideline and on a line. The defender takes off from the sideline as if approaching the kickoff line. At this point, the stopwatch is started and the drill is videotaped. The defender weaves through the dummies, staying tight to them without his shoulder pads touching the dummies. The dip-and-rip technique is used. As the defender approaches the shield holders, the first two holders will execute a double-team. The defender will split the double-team, maintain balance, and rapidly approach the next pair of shield holders. On a signal given by a coach, one of the next two shield holders attacks the defender (to simulate reading the upfield shoulder). After the defender properly avoids opposite (i.e., reads the upfield shoulder), the defender will step over two low agile bags and immediately come to balance. As the defender steps over the last agile bag, the ballcarrier runs upfield for three yards and angle runs. The defender must make the proper angle tackle. When the tackle is made properly, the stopwatch is stopped, the video recorder is paused, and times are recorded.

Coaching Points:

- A blocker can be used in front of the ballcarrier to simulate the hardhat area with a shock-and-lock technique and a dip-and-rip escape.
- The shield holders can change the type of block, with the first set of holders simulating the upfield shoulder read and the second set using the double-team.

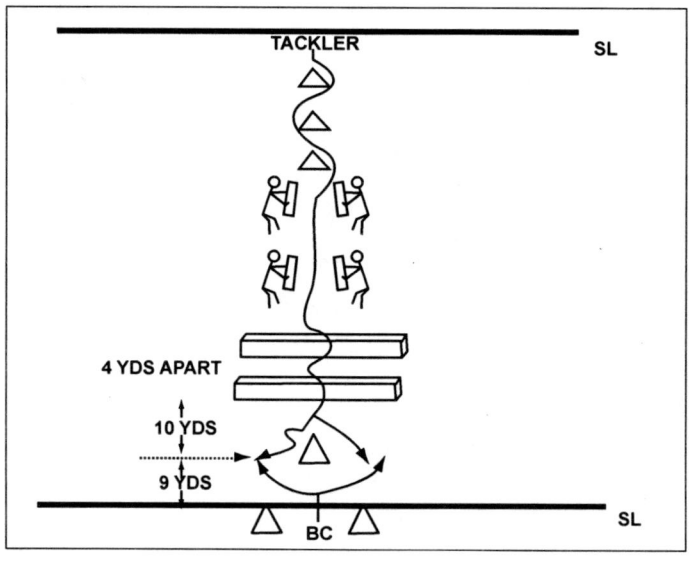

#8: Combo Kickoff Coverage vs. Cross or Angle Blocks (Individual)

Objective: To concentrate on perfecting the technique of avoiding the front line on a kickoff return and encountering angle blocks on the second line of blocking

Equipment Needed: Dots, shields

Description: The defender takes off and stays in his lane for the first 10 yards. The defender must avoid the first block (the blocker should turn his shoulders or do a short fishhook) by using quick feet, reading the upfield shoulder, and using a dip-and-rip technique. Once the first blocker is cleared and the defender gets back into his lane, he continues to read the blocks of the second line. On the go command, one blocker will angle toward the defender to block him. The defender must avoid the blocker who is coming on an angle, and must destroy the upfield shoulder. Once the defender is in the process of reading the upfield shoulder, the ballcarrier starts upfield on an angle and the defender runs parallel to the ballcarrier, keeping the shoulders square. The defender continues to approach the ballcarrier and makes a proper angle tackle.

Coaching Points:

- This drill should be performed at full speed.
- Make sure the defender stays in his lane and does not drift.

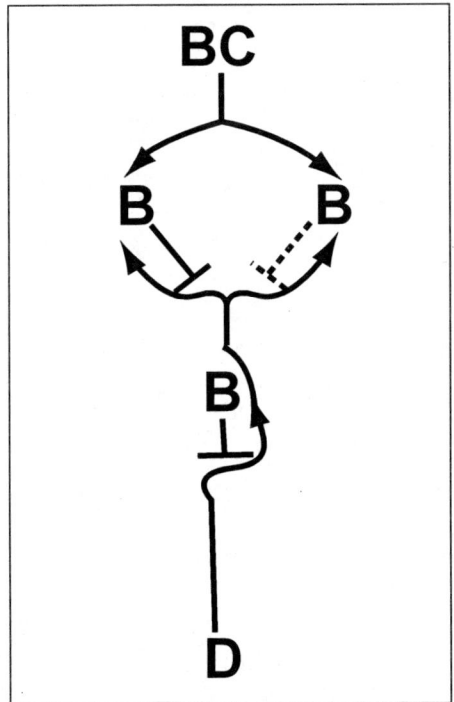

#9: Combo Kickoff Coverage vs. Double-Team Blocks (Individual)

Objective: To perfect the techniques needed to avoid the front line and encounter double-team by the second line

Equipment Needed: Shields

Description: The defenders and blockers move on a go command. The defender takes off and stays in his lane for the first 10 yards. The blockers perform their fishhooks, attacking simultaneously to form the double-team. The defender must split through the double-team using a dip-and-rip technique and maintaining his balance. The defender continues to approach the ballcarrier and makes a proper angle tackle.

Coaching Points:

- Schemes should include angle blocking and double-teaming.
- The blockers can hold shields or perform live.

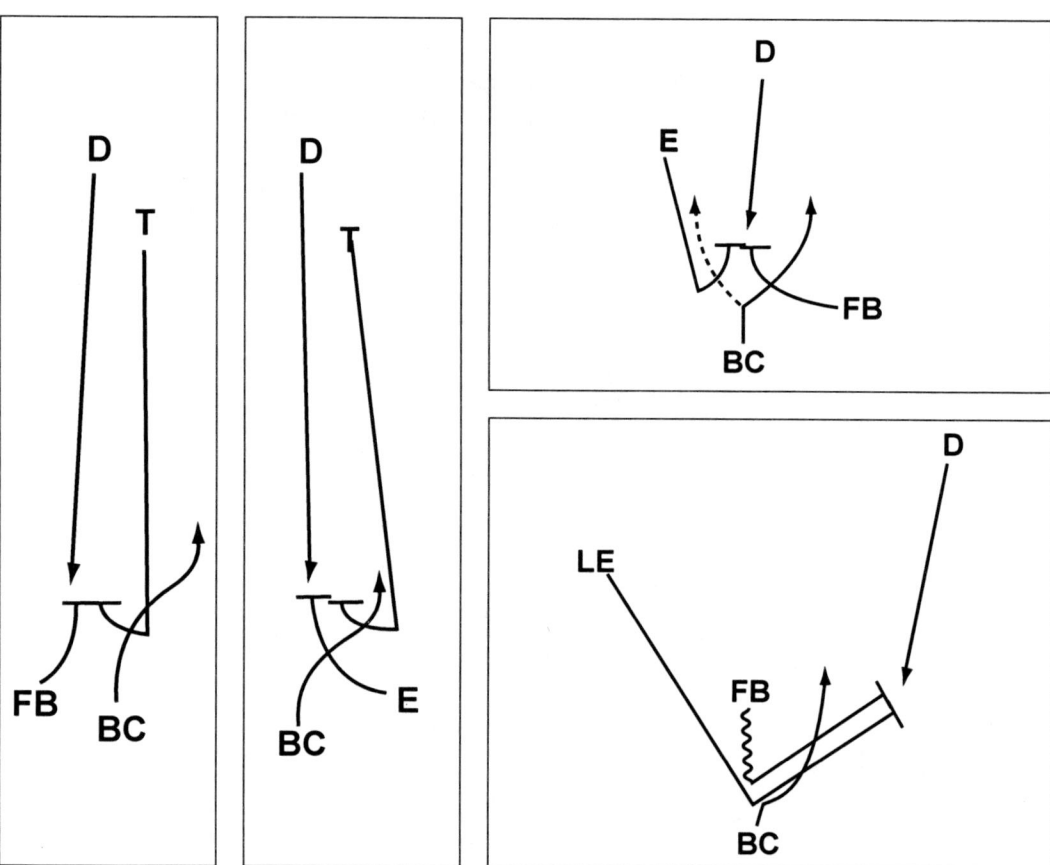

#10: Combo Kickoff Coverage vs. Drive Blocks (Individual)

Objective: To destroy face-up blocks as the defender gets closer to the ballcarrier

Equipment Needed: Dots, shields

Description: The defender takes off and stays in his lane for the first 10 yards. The defender must avoid the first block (the blocker should turn his shoulders or do a short fishhook) by using quick feet, reading the upfield shoulder, and using a dip-and-rip technique. Once the first blocker is cleared and the defender gets back into his lane, he continues to read the blocks of the second line. A single shield holder that is aligned in front of the ballcarrier blocks straight ahead. The defender uses a butt-and-press move (shock-and-lock technique) to drive the blocker back, uses a dip-and-rip to escape, and then tackles the ballcarrier.

Coaching Points:

- The second blocker can swing his hips between the defender and the ballcarrier.
- This drill should be performed at full speed.
- Make sure the defender stays in his lane and does not drift.

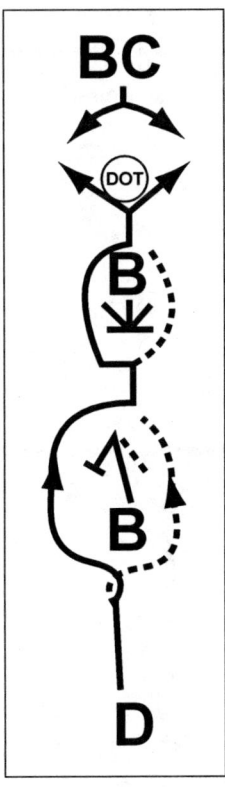

#11: Kickoff Coverage vs. Wideside Blocking Schemes (Group)

Objective: To utilize techniques that destroy various blocking schemes during kickoff returns

Equipment Needed: Scout look card (developed based on opponents' blocking schemes) with kickoff return blocking schemes

Description: Utilizing half of the kickoff coverage personnel on the wideside and the return players that are responsible for blocking on the wideside, the return team follows the scheme drawn on the scout look card. The drill starts with the ball being kicked to initiate the blocking scheme and coverage responsibilities. The defenders start straight down the field for 10 yards at full speed, reading the upfield shoulder of the first-line defenders and looking at the second-line blocking scheme. Utilizing the proper techniques (i.e., angle, double-team, and drive), blocks will be attacked. Once the blocks have been destroyed, the coverage team will leverage the ballcarrier and proceed to tackle the returner and attempt to create a turnover.

Coaching Point: Schemes should include angle blocking, crossers, and double-teams that key perimeter personnel would use during kickoff returns.

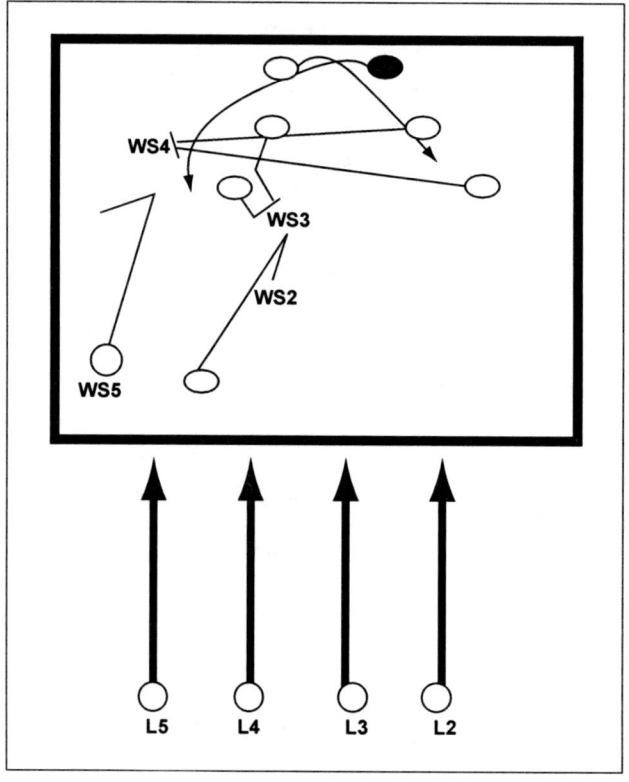

#12: Wedge Breakup (Group)

Objective: To develop skills for the players that are responsible for attacking a wedge during a kickoff return

Equipment Needed: Scout look cards (developed based on opponents' blocking schemes)

Description: Utilizing half of the kickoff coverage personnel on the wideside and the return players that are responsible for blocking on the wideside, the return team follows the scheme drawn on the scout look card. The drill starts with the ball being kicked to initiate the blocking scheme and coverage responsibilities. The defenders start straight down the field for 10 yards at full speed, reading the upfield shoulder and looking at the second-line blocking scheme. The wedge forms and slowly moves up the field. The kickoff coverage team seeks their individual gap responsibilities and destroys the wedge-blocking scheme using the proper techniques and butt and press (shock and lock). Once a defender busts the wedge, he comes to balance, locates the ballcarrier, and proceeds to make a proper angle tackle.

Coaching Point: The wedge buster must understand what gap he is responsible for and the force responsibilities he has.

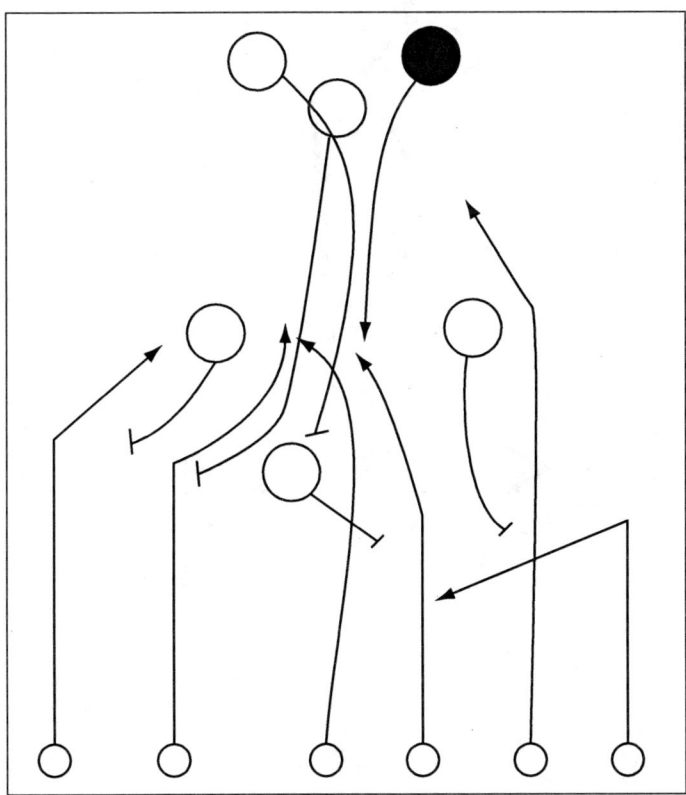

#13: Beat the Cross-Block (Group)

Objective: To teach kickoff coverage personnel how to avoid cross-blocks while maintaining lane leverage

Equipment Needed: Scout look cards (developed based on opponents' blocking schemes)

Description: Kickoff coverage and return players align according to the diagram. On the go command, players begin running in their cross lanes and cross-blocking. As the cross-blocker enters the defender's lane, the defender, using foot fakes, sets up the blockers and then crosses over tightly around the upfield shoulder. Once clear from the blocker, the defender readjusts back to the proper lane.

Coaching Point: The cross-blocks should be performed to the right and left and with other combinations (e.g., cross-block and double-team).

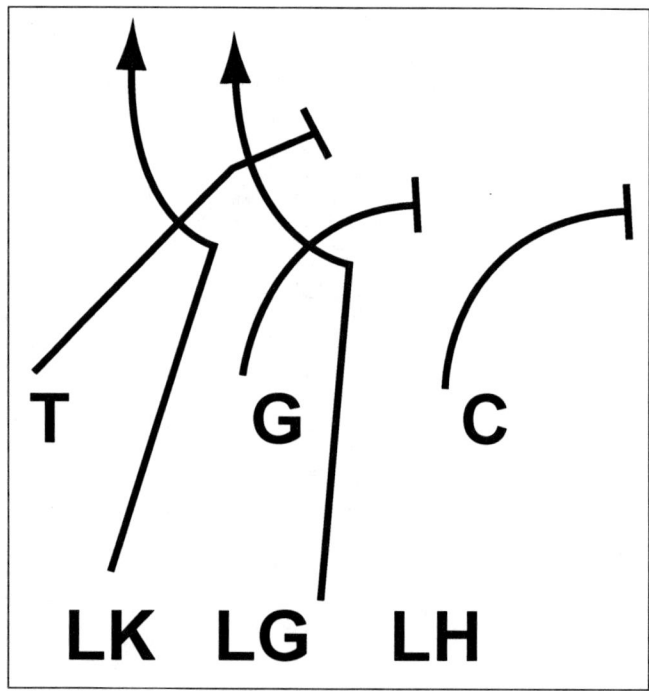

#14: Team Leverage (Team)

Objective: To install the major components of kickoff coverage (i.e., taking off, maintaining lanes, reading the upfield shoulder, destroying blocks, coming to balance, and leveraging the ball)

Equipment Needed: Kicker, ball

Description: Utilizing a full kickoff coverage team, the defenders take off with the kicker approaching the ball. On the return side there are two blockers for each coverage player. The first blocker fishhooks right or left. This movement enables an upfield shoulder read. The second blocker attacks the defender with shock and lock. The defender presses back the blocker and reads the ballcarrier. There are two returners ready to be the ballcarrier waiting in the end zone. One returner that has been preselected by a coach will wait for five seconds before moving up the field and then going laterally. The defender uses a dip-and-rip technique to escape, comes to balance, and leverages the ballcarrier.

Coaching Points:

- The defenders must go full speed and maintain their lanes.
- The defenders keep the ball leveraged inside out.
- The drill can also be run with fewer lines.

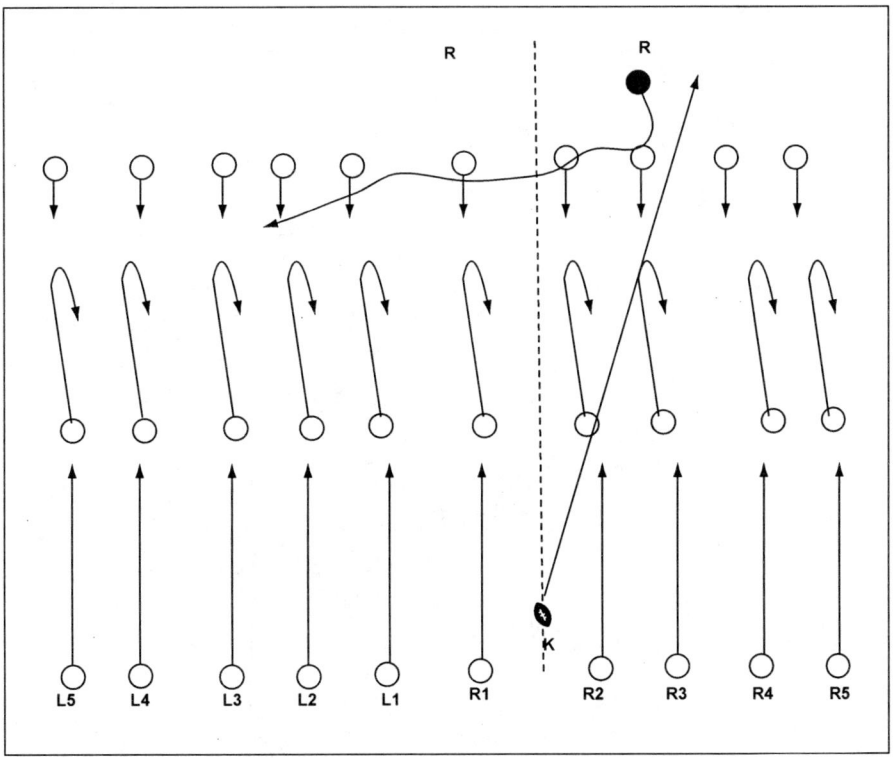

#15: Kickoff Coverage vs. Scout (Team)

Objective: To incorporate scheme reading and techniques on kickoff coverage versus kickoff return team

Equipment Needed: Scout look cards (developed based on opponents' blocking schemes)

Description: The kickoff coverage team takes off with the ball being kicked. The kickoff return team executes their blocks as per assignment. (The diagrams show examples of different kickoff return schemes that may be used.) The returner runs the ball back according to the plan. The kickoff coverage team reacts to blocks and leverages the ballcarrier.

Coaching Point: This drill should be performed at full speed by the kickoff return team and at three-quarter speed by the kickoff coverage team to make sure that all the fits are proper.

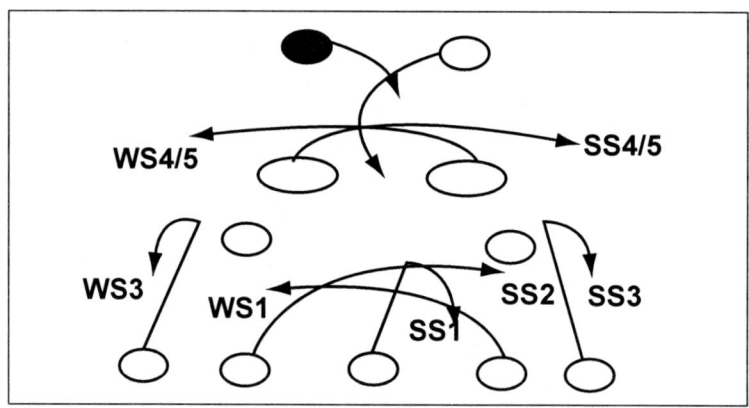

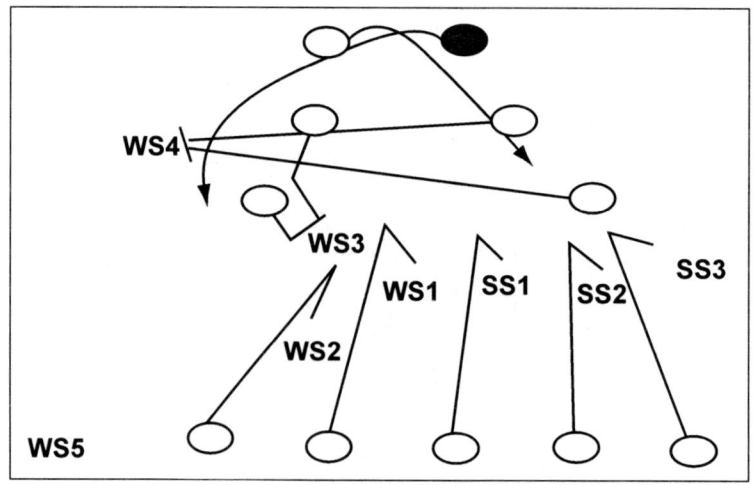

2

Skill Development for Blocking Kickoff Returns

#16: Fishhook—Sprint, Backpedal, Gather, Come Out (Individual)

Objective: To teach the proper mechanics for each phase of a fishhook block

Equipment Needed: Cones

Description: Arrange cones to create lanes for 20 yards. The player should align facing in an angle anticipating a kickoff. When the ball is kicked (visual key), he springs into action by crossing over and sprinting to the landmark. The landmarks will be 20 yards downfield. As the player approaches the landmark at 17 yards, he backpedals for three yards and pushes off his back foot. Once his foot is planted, the player works up on an angle and cha-chas his feet to the block point.

Coaching Point: As the player sprints downfield, he needs to peek upfield to locate his blocking assignment (pistol position).

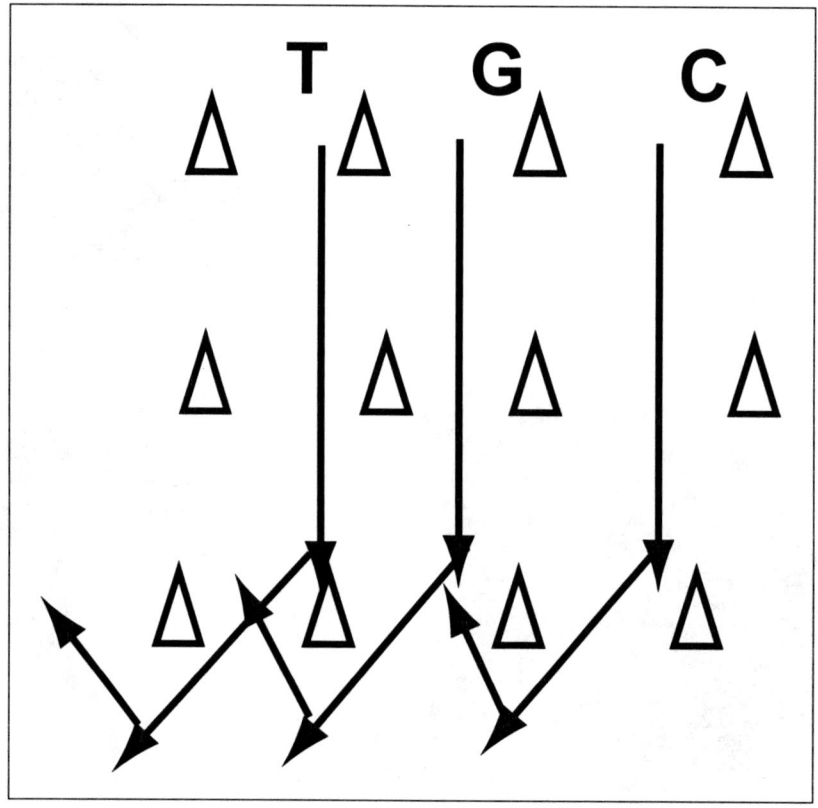

#17: Punch and Drive (Individual)

Objective: To teach the proper hand placement and foot movement for blocking on a kickoff return

Equipment Needed: Shields

Description: A defender holding a shield should stand three yards away from a blocker. On a coach's command, the blocker and the defender run toward each other. The blocker punches the defender with a hand jam, runs his feet, and locks out his arms, driving the blocker back.

Coaching Point: Right and left calls may be added to have the blocker turn his hips with his foot movement to simulate protecting the running lane.

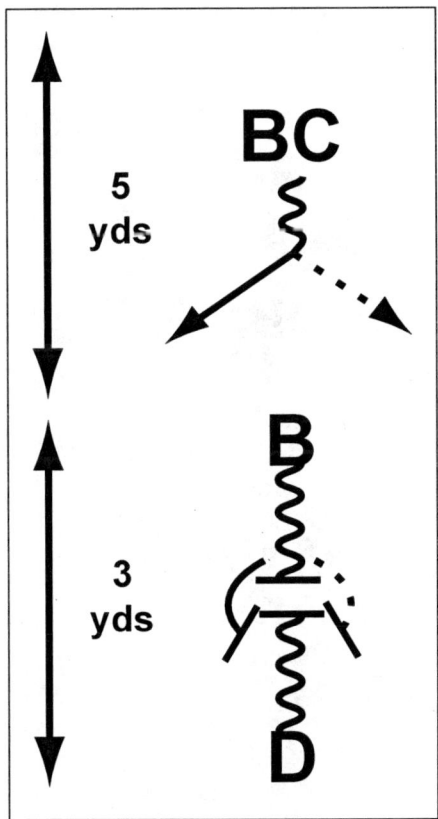

#18: Steer (Individual)

Objective: To improve the ability of the blocker to maintain contact with the defender as the ballcarrier moves up the field

Equipment Needed: None

Description: The blocker and the defender start in a proper fit position (lock up). The blocker's hands are inside the defender's hands. On the go command, the blocker and defender run their feet, and the defender attempts to escape using a pass-rush move or moving laterally. The blocker maintains contact by running his feet, replacing his hands, and positioning his hips behind the defender and ballcarrier.

Coaching Points:

- More than one pair can be doing this drill at the same time.
- A running back can be added to create a more competitive, game-situation drill.

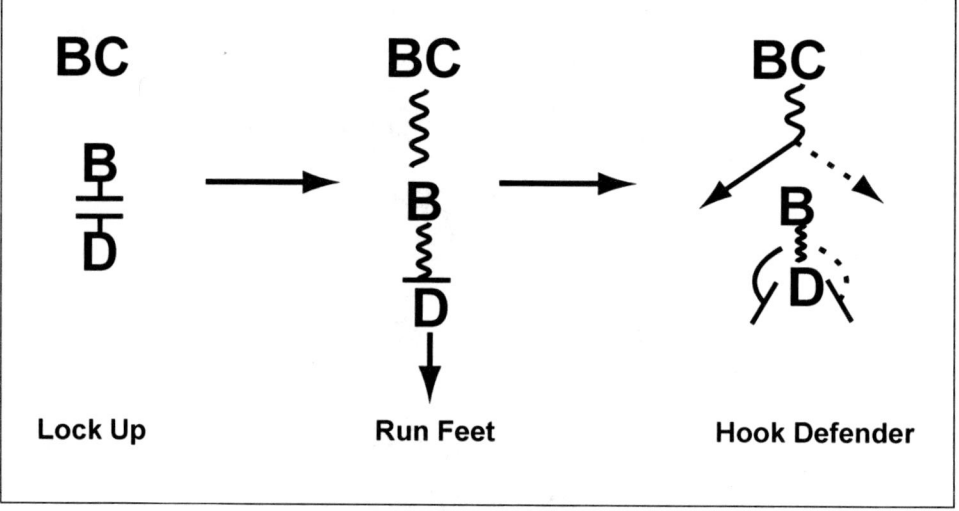

#19: Sprint, Gather, Finish (Individual)

Objective: To develop all phases of the fishhook technique used to block on kickoff returns

Equipment Needed: Cones

Description: The drill is set up the same as #16: Fishhook, with defenders (D) added to each lane (Diagram A). The drill commences with a go command. The defenders run their coverage lanes and the blockers (T, G, C) spring into action, sprinting to the landmark (17 to 20 yards). Then, the blockers backpedal, gather, and push off the deeper foot, working up to the defender. Upon contact, the blocker punches, drives, and steers the defender.

Coaching Points:

- This drill must be performed to the right and to the left.
- Adding a returner and having the defender try to tackle the returner will help enhance the ability of the blocker to maintain leverage on the defender.
- After the blockers have learned the proper technique, modify the drill to simulate a more openfield, game-like situation (Diagram B). Have the coverage players (3, 2, 1 in Diagram B) cross lanes to teach blockers how to handle crossers.

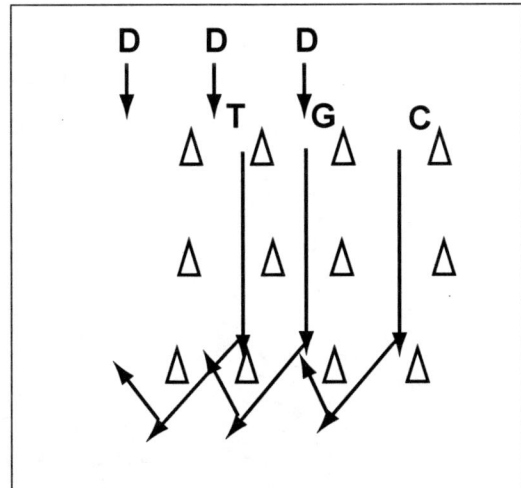

Diagram A

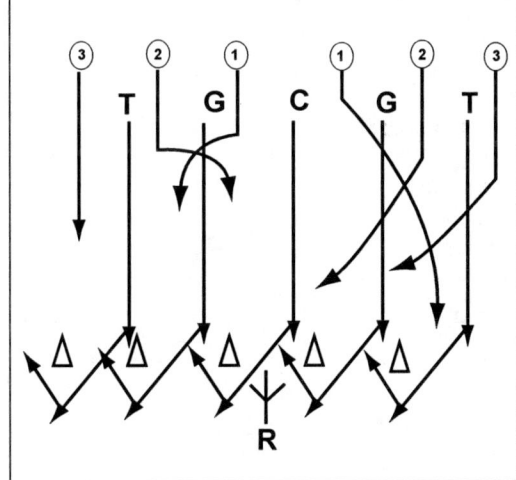

Diagram B

#20: Kickoff Coverage/Return Evaluation (Individual)

Objective: To enhance the ability of the coverage team to attack the blocker and the return team to block using fishhook techniques

Equipment Needed: Cones, football

Description: Align the cones as coverage lanes and have the kickoff returner's front-line players align according to scheme. A defender is placed 10 yards away on top of each blocker. A returner is placed downfield to receive the kick. The defender starts his motion with the kicker's approach to the football. The front-line blocker makes sure the ball is kicked and begins his fishhook. The blocker sets the angle as he peeks at the ball in flight and turns back to locate the defender. The blocker sprints to his landmark and works up to the defender. The defender attempts to get to the ballcarrier. The blocker must use all of the techniques to block the defender or maintain proper leverage to keep the running lane open.

Coaching Points:

- Have the returner move upfield when the defender is five yards from the blocker.
- As an optional drill, the defenders can cover in multiples and the blocker and returner could work on various return schemes.

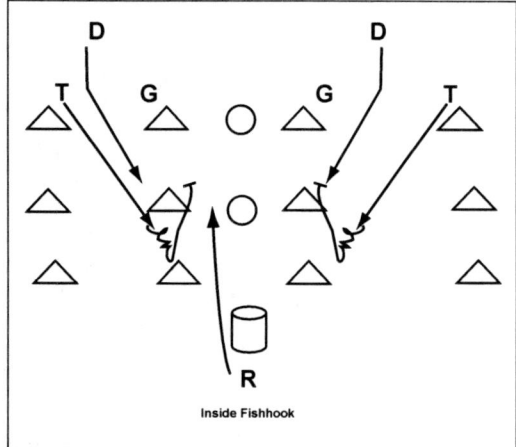

Inside Fishhook

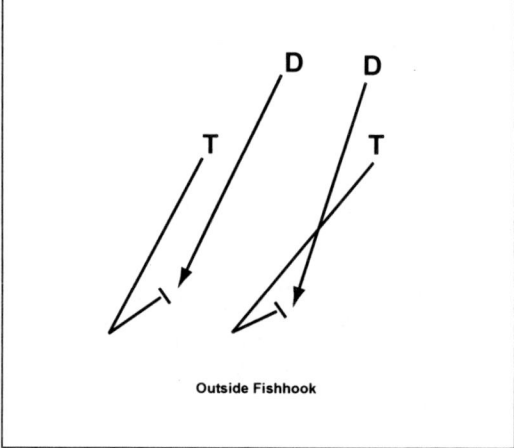

Outside Fishhook

#21: Shoot and Run or Retrace (Individual)

Objective: To improve the ability of the front-line players on the kickoff return to sustain angle blocks

Equipment Needed: Cones

Description: Players should align according to the diagram. On the go command, the kickoff coverage player (D) runs downfield. The return team blocker performs a fishhook. As the players approach each other, the coverage player sets his sights on tackling the ballcarrier. The coverage player can avoid with a hard turn or crossover (reading the upfield shoulder). The blocker must ride or retrace the defender.

Coaching Point: The fishhooks should be performed to the right and to the left with both hard turns and retrace moves by the defenders.

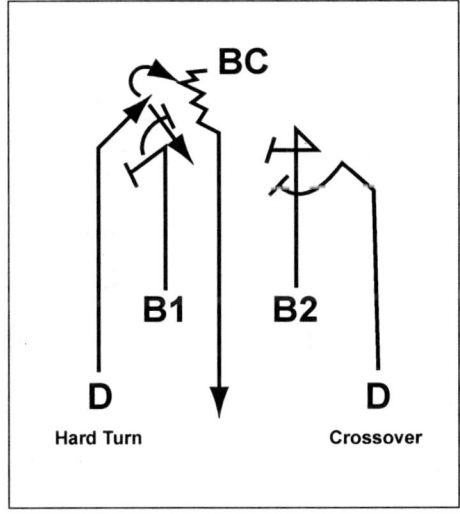

#22: Cross-Blocks (Group)

Objective: To develop the ability to coordinate cross-blocking and maintain leverage on blocking the defender

Equipment Needed: Scout look cards (developed based on opponents' kickoff coverage schemes), football

Description: Front-line kickoff players should align according to the return scheme. Provide enough coverage players to accommodate the return's cross-blocking scheme. On command, the defenders run downfield in their coverage lanes. The front-line players sprint in their cross-blocking scheme and block their individual assignments.

Coaching Points:

- Have the defenders stay in their lane and hard turn or read the upfield shoulder and cross over.
- Add a ballcarrier returning the football up the middle to provide game-like conditions.

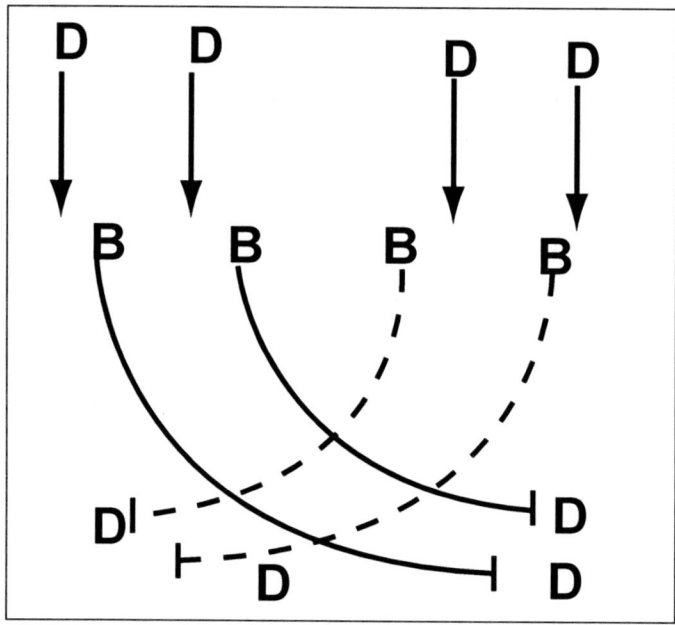

3

Skill Development
for Punt Pressure

#23: Get Off and Bend (Individual)

Objective: To teach the punt pressure personnel the concept that getting off, staying low, and bending properly enhances the opportunities for blocking kicks

Equipment Needed: Chute, cones, football

Description: Utilizing a lineman's chute and placing the cones as shown in the diagram, align the rushers on the line of scrimmage slightly under the chute. On the center's simulated snap, each rusher performs a get-off, exploding under the chute, bending with a plant on the outside foot at the first cone, dipping the inside shoulder, pointing the inside foot toward the block point, and ripping with the inside arm. As the rusher runs past the last cone, his arms and hands should extend properly to block the kick.

Coaching Points:

- Perform the drill to the right or to the left.
- A coach or player could hold a soft ball to simulate the ball on the kicker's foot.
- Timing the drill helps with identifying potential punt block specialists.

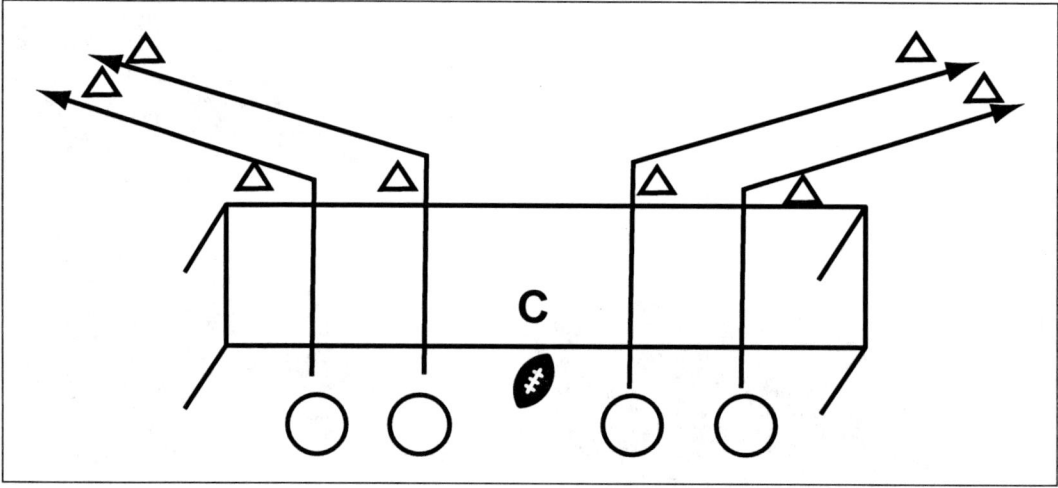

#24: Maintain Low Pad Level (Individual)

Objective: To enhance the technique of staying low and keeping the shoulder pads under the blocker when rushing the punter

Equipment Needed: Shields, football

Description: The center simulates a snap and a rusher explodes off the line of scrimmage. Another player stands two yards away holding a shield. As the rusher approaches the blocker (shield holder), the blocker lightly pushes the shield down on the rusher. The rusher must keep his shoulder pads under the shield, plant his outside foot, dip and rip, and explode to the block point.

Coaching Points:

- A player can be on a knee at the block point with a soft ball being presented so that the rusher uses proper hand placement to block the ball down.
- Two rushers from each side do the drill simultaneously with one side being a scoop-and-score player. After the soft ball is batted down, the scoop-and-score player recovers the ball and sprints upfield.

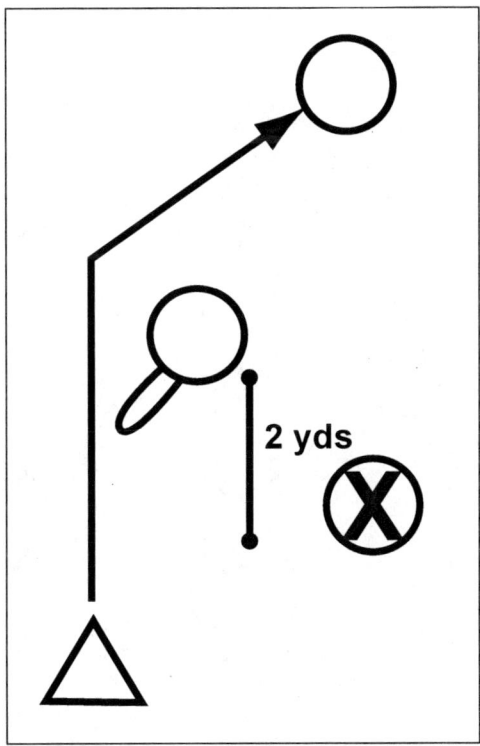

#25: Run the Hoop (Individual)

Objective: To teach punt pressure players the proper approach to block a kick based on the punter's foot and takeoff alignment

Equipment Needed: Hoops, football

Description: Place five hoops as shown in the diagram and space them out according to the alignment of the punt unit. On the snap of the ball, one rusher takes off toward the punter using the proper rush techniques (i.e., get-off, bend) that have been developed in previous drills. This drill is a rapid-fire drill that goes down the line. If the punter is right-footed, the outside rushers on both sides and the inside rusher away from the punter's kicking leg cross over the punter's leg. The inside rusher to the kicker's foot must get to the block point turned sideways (i.e., parallel to the kicker's leg) to avoid the kicking leg.

Coaching Points:

- Make sure players use the proper block techniques with the hands and body, and correct as needed.
- This drill can be timed for selection of personnel.

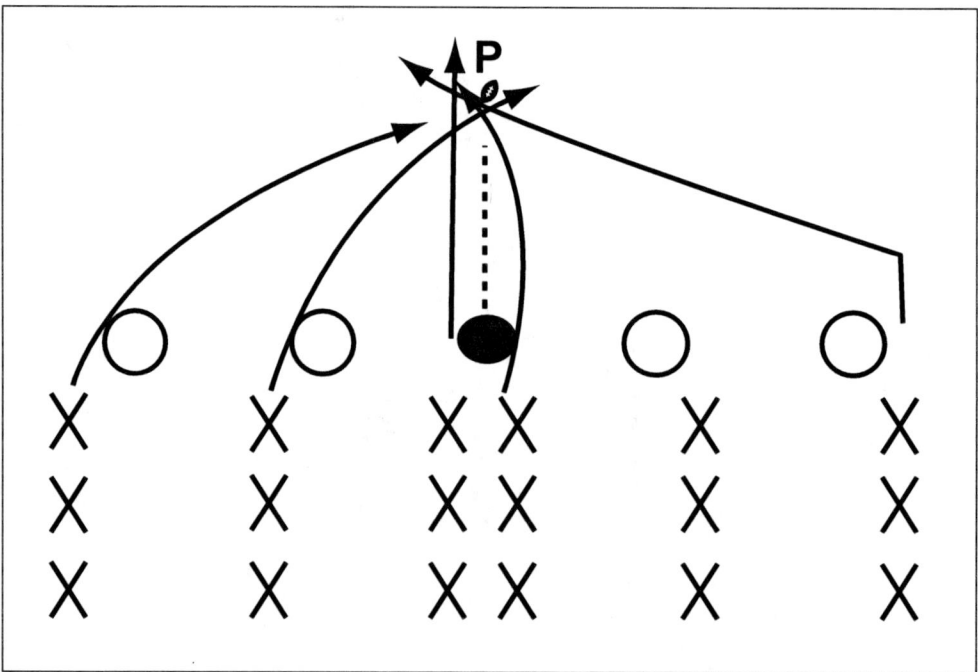

#26: Drive and Come to Balance (Individual)

Objective: To improve the ability of the punt pressure player to maintain his block on the punt defender as long as possible during the punt return phase

Equipment Needed: None

Description: Have the defender either fit to a blocker or have the defender get off the line of scrimmage on the snap of the ball and meet the blocker. The blocker will execute a kick-slide (zone protection) or man protection technique. The defender will use his hands and execute a butt-and-press technique (shock and lock) on the blocker, running his feet and driving the blocker back. The more the blocker gets driven back, the wider the feet go to create a sound base (cha-cha feet). When the blocker escapes, the defender drops his hands immediately, comes to balance, turns, and looks for the returner and the ball position, which establish the trail and fit path for the defender. The defender runs with the blocker for 10 yards in an off-trail technique, not contacting the blocker and eyeing the position of the returner to maintain the trail path.

Coaching Point: The defender must keep his hips and shoulders square to the blocker until the blocker tries to escape. At that point, the defender immediately drops his hands, turns, looks downfield, and runs.

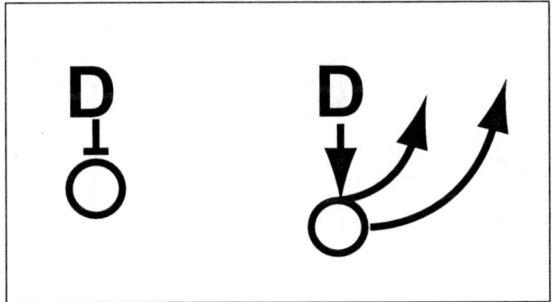

#27: Trail (Individual)

Objective: To teach the proper off-trail mechanics and blocking techniques for a successful punt return

Equipment Needed: Football

Description: Set up the drill as shown in the diagram with two groups executing the drill at the same time. The punt pressure personnel is aligned one to two yards behind the coverage person. On the go command, both players sprint down the field to a cone (approximately 20 yards). When the players are halfway to the cone, the coach in the center flips the ball to the returner. The defender now closes in on the ballcarrier. The punt pressure blocker wheels on the defender and jams the chest with his hands. His hips and shoulders should now be perpendicular to the defender's shoulder pad. He should keep his feet moving to keep the defender from escaping the block.

Coaching Points:

- Don't have blockers come in contact with the defender down the field.
- When the defender closes, the blocker needs to spring into action.
- The blocker maintains his leverage by peeking at the position of the returner and the defender for timing of the block.

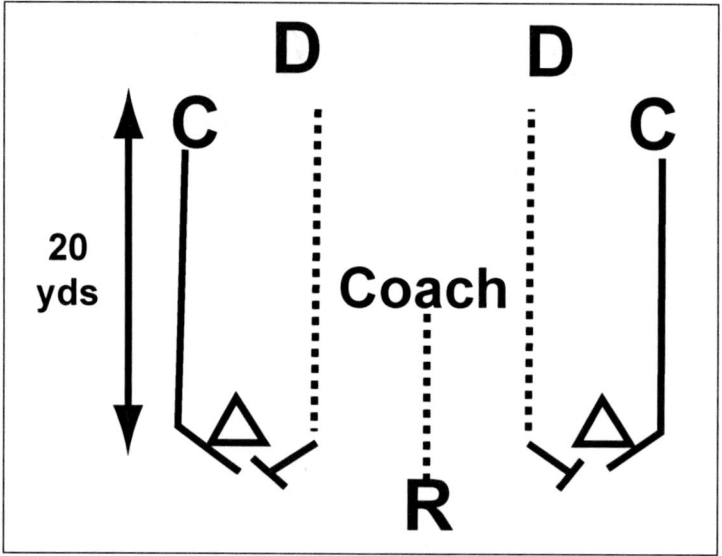

#28: Retrace (Individual)

Objective: To teach the punt pressure player to block when the coverage player stops and comes back over the top to tackle the punt returner

Equipment Needed: Football

Description: This drill is set up and executed the same as Drill #27: Trail. The difference in this drill occurs when the defender attempts to close on the returner. As the defender hits his landmark to close, he stops and works over the top. The punt pressure blocker needs to either zone turn or man turn (defensive back technique) to retrace his position and block the defender as described in Drill #27: Trail.

Coaching Points:

- The punt pressure blocker must keep his eyes on the defender and the returner to set the point of the block and know when to retrace.
- Blockers should never overrun the defender.

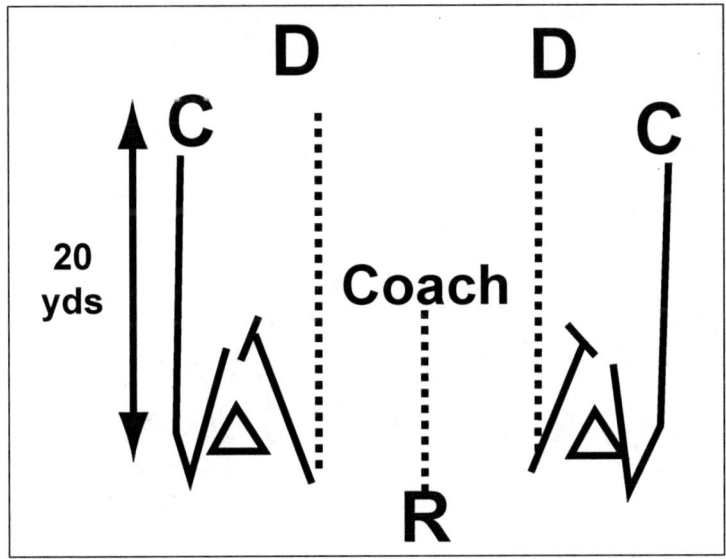

#29: Pods (Group/Team)

Objective: To improve the techniques of punt pressure personnel based on the return scheme

Equipment Needed: Football

Description: A scout punt team is assembled based on an opponent's alignment. The scout team is instructed to use the opponent's blocking scheme and techniques. The punt pressure team aligns according to their scheme and uses the proper technique to execute their assignment. The drill is broken down into three segments: stinger and swatters, last two players outside of the interior, and the rest of the players from the interior. Both the right and left sides of each group go together. Using a pre-determined script, the coach signals one group to go. On the center's snap of the ball, the selected group springs into action according to the scheme, and both units execute their proper techniques. The punter kicks and the returner catches the football. The returner reads the coverage, finding his running lane and moving the ball upfield.

Coaching Point: This drill can be used to work on returners catching the football under pressure as well as developing wall punt returns, depending on the scheme.

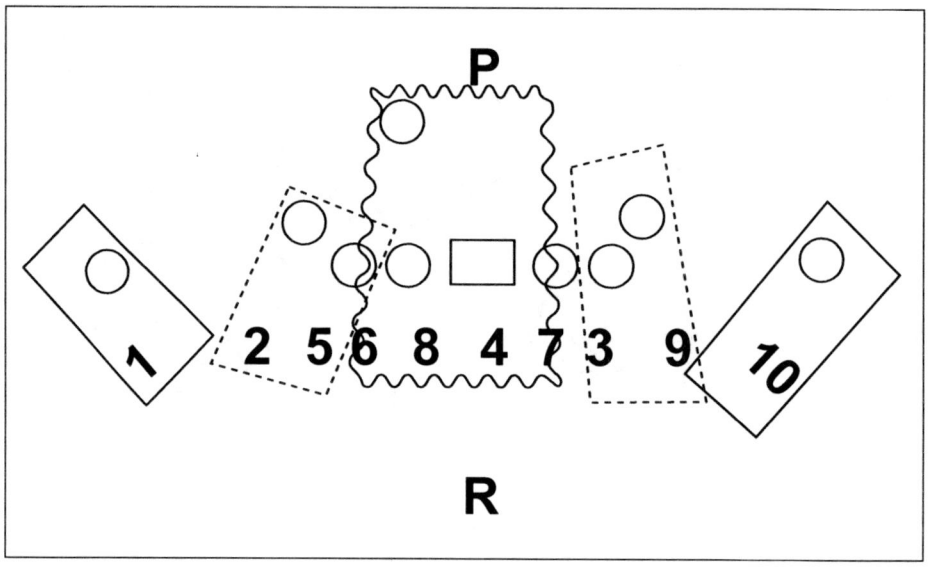

#30: Wall and Mirror (Group/Team)

Objective: To develop the technique for blocking on a wall punt return

Description: The wall (return) and coverage (punt) personnel should align as shown in the diagram. On the snap, the wall players take off and drive the blockers back (pre-set wall). They should place their hands on the breastplate and widen their feet slightly while driving the blocker back. When the blocker escapes, the wall players should drop their hands, maintain balance, and run to form a wall. The first wall player downfield should work at least five to seven yards wider than the returner, working toward the returner. The remaining wall personnel should be spaced five yards apart and also work toward the returner. As the coverage personnel close in on the returner and run to tackle the returner, the wall personnel position themselves to block in front of and above the waist of the coverage personnel. They should place their eyes on the defender's numbers, shoot their hands inside to the defender's chest, reset their hands if needed, widen their feet, sink their hips, stay low, and steer the defender away from the returner's path (mirror).

Coaching Point: Add a return from a live kick from different areas (right and left hash mark) on the field to aid in setting the wall properly.

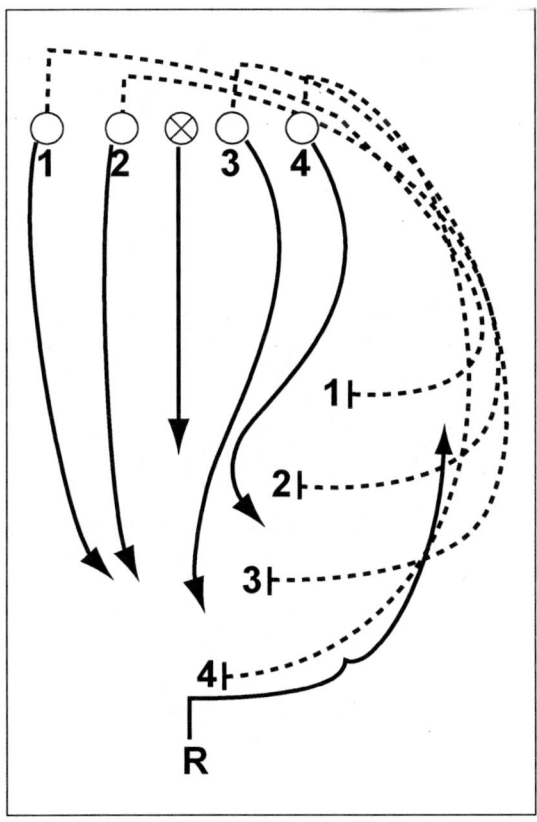

4

Strength & Conditioning for Punters and Kickers

#31: Warm-Up and Stretching

Objective: To provide maximum flexibility in the core power areas (i.e., hamstrings, quadriceps, buttocks, hip flexors, groin, calves, and the lower back)

Equipment Needed: None

Description: Kickers and punters must stretch regularly in order to improve their techniques. A flexible kicker or punter is able to maximize his ability by being able to explode up through the ball on each and every kick and punt. Flexibility helps prevent nagging injuries that can occur over the course of a season.

Warm-up:

- One lap around the football field or five minutes on a stationary bike
- High-knee pumps across the field or 15 seconds standing in place
- Butt kicks across the field or 15 seconds in place
- High knee skips across the field and back or 15 seconds standing in place

Stretches:

- *Straight-leg hang (hamstrings):* The athlete relaxes and bends at the waist, trying to touch his palms to the ground. He should keep his knees completely straight. He stretches each leg individually by crossing one leg over the other (right over left, then left over right).
- *Leg V (hamstrings):* Sitting on the ground, the athlete spreads his legs as wide as possible. Keeping his legs straight and his toes pointed upward, he should lower his chest to his right thigh with his head and eyes looking forward. He then lowers his chest between his legs to stretch both hamstrings. Finally, he repeats the stretch over the left thigh.
- *Modified hurdler's stretch (hamstrings and lower back):* The athlete should sit with one leg out straight and the other leg bent in with the bottom part of the foot touching the inner thigh of the straight leg. He reaches out and grabs his big toe on the straight leg with his hand. He then switches sides and repeats.
- *Butterfly (groin and hip flexors):* From a sitting position, the athlete places the soles of his feet together. He pulls his ankles as close to his groin as possible. He grabs his ankles with his hands and uses his elbows to push his knees to the ground. Then, to stretch the hip flexors, he pushes his heels out farther away from his body and pulls his chest down and out toward his feet by grabbing his ankles.
- *Pretzel (back and buttocks):* The athlete sits on the ground with both legs straight out. Keeping flat on the ground, he bends his left leg toward his body. He raises his right leg and crosses it over the top of his left leg, placing the bottom of his right foot flat on the ground to the outside of his thigh. He twists his upper body so that he is looking over his shoulder behind himself, using his left arm to push against his right thigh for rotation help. He repeats this stretch to the opposite side.

- *Lying/seated knee grab (glutes and hip flexors):* The athlete lies flat on his back, pulls his right knee up toward his chest until he feels the stretch, and holds. He repeats this stretch with his left leg. From a seated position, he can also pull his right knee up toward his chest until he feels a stretch. By varying the position of his leg, he will stretch either his glutes or his hip flexors.
- *Back roll (back):* The athlete pulls his knees to his chest and holds them tight. He rocks back and forth on the small portion of his lower back. To further stretch the lower back and legs, he flips his legs back over his head until they touch the ground behind him.
- *Kneeling quadriceps (quadriceps):* From a kneeling position, the athlete puts one leg out in front of him so that his knee forms a 90-degree angle. He leans back slightly to stretch the front quadriceps on the leg that is down.
- *Squat (groin and hip flexors):* Keeping his feet flat on the ground and his toes slightly bent outward, the athlete squats down. He places his elbows on the inside of his knees and, keeping his hands together, pushes out.
- *Calf stretch (calves):* The athlete places his hands on the ground out in front of him and puts one leg back behind him flat on the ground with the other leg over top of the calf being stretched.
- *Standing quad stretch (quadriceps):* Standing on his left leg, the athlete grabs his right ankle and pulls it back as far toward his buttocks as possible and holds. He switches legs and repeats the stretch.

Dynamic Extension:

- *Rockettes (10 each leg):* The athlete lies with his back flat on the ground and his hands out to the side. He brings his right foot to his left hand and then does the opposite.
- *Back kicks (10 each leg):* The athlete lies with his stomach flat on the ground and his hands out to the side. He brings his right foot to his left hand and then does the opposite.
- *Balanced swings (10 each leg):* Balancing on his left leg with his arms out to the side, the athlete swings his right leg up as far as possible to meet his left hand out in front of him. He switches legs and repeats the stretch.
- *Frankensteins:* The athlete walks 20 yards with stiff legs, kicking up his foot to his opposite outstretched hand.
- *Walking lunge with twists:* With his hands on his head, the athlete performs a forward lunge with the left leg and brings his right elbow to his left knee for 20 yards. He repeats the stretch with the opposite leg, and continues alternating lunges.

Coaching Points:

- Make sure that the kickers and punters are fully warmed up before stretching.
- Make sure they do not *bounce*, but rather *hold* each stretch for 20 seconds.

STRENGTH TRAINING

The key to these drills, just as in kicking and punting, is to emphasize *techniques*. Slow, controlled movements during the lifting section and where noted is essential. Have the athletes start with lighter weights, which allows them to focus on perfecting techniques. Then, have them increase the weight. Most of the exercises do not require using any weight. Kickers and punters need to focus on using less weight and doing more repetitions. The routines should be varied from time to time to prevent a plateau effect. Also, they should give their bodies the time they need for rest and recuperation between workouts.

#32: Back Squats (Upper and Lower Legs)

Objective: To promote muscular strength, power, and endurance in order to increase leg speed

Equipment Needed: Barbell with weight plates

Description: The athlete should position a barbell on his lower neck area, keeping his focus up and out in front of him. He grips the bar with his hands close to shoulder-width apart, with his elbows pushed up and in. He stands with his feet shoulder-width apart, his chest and buttocks out, and his knees slightly bent. He slowly descends by pushing his hips back and flexing at his hip and knee joints, going down until his thighs are parallel to the ground. He drives out of the bottom by extending his knee and hip joints.

Coaching Point: Make sure the athlete keeps his chest and head up while maintaining a tight arch in his back and his weight on his heels.

#33: Front Squats (Upper and Lower Legs)

Objective: To promote muscular strength, power, and endurance in order to increase leg speed

Equipment Needed: Barbell with weight plates

Description: The athlete places a barbell in front of him, just above his chest. He folds his arms across his chest and the bar to help keep his balance and to keep the bar in place. He stands with his feet shoulder-width apart, his chest and buttocks out, and his knees slightly bent. He slowly descends by pushing his hips back and flexing at his hip and knee joints, going down until his thighs are parallel to the ground.

Coaching Point: The athlete should use less weight for the front squats than he did in #32: Back Squats, and he should focus on improving his balance.

#34: Split Squats (Upper and Lower Legs)

Objective: To promote muscular strength, power, and endurance in order to increase leg speed

Equipment Needed: Barbell with weight plates

Description: This drill is similar to #32: Back Squats, only the legs are split. The athlete should position a barbell on his lower neck area and keep his focus up and out in front of him. He grips the bar with his hands close to shoulder-width apart, with his elbows pushed up and in. He stands with one foot forward, his chest and buttocks out, and his knees slightly bent. He slowly descends until his lead thigh is parallel to the ground. He rises up and, after a prescribed number of repetitions, repeats the exercise with the opposite leg in front.

Coaching Point: Make sure the knee of the athlete's lead leg does not go past his toes.

#35: Squat Jumps (Upper and Lower Legs)

Objective: To promote muscular strength, power, and endurance in order to increase leg speed

Equipment Needed: Barbell with weight plates

Description: The athlete should position a barbell on his lower neck area and keep his focus up and out in front of him. He grips the bar with his hands close to shoulder-width apart, with his elbows pushed up and in. He stands with his feet shoulder-width apart, his chest and buttocks out, and his knees slightly bent. He slowly descends by pushing his hips back and flexing at his hip and knee joints, going down until his thighs are parallel to the ground. He drives out of the bottom by extending his knee and hip joints and jumping up in the air.

Coaching Point: The athlete should focus on a soft landing while working on his balance and coordination.

#36: Overhead Squats (Upper and Lower Legs)

Objective: To promote muscular strength, power, and endurance in order to increase leg speed

Equipment Needed: Barbell with weight plates

Description: The athlete should position his hands on a barbell in a snatch grip position (i.e., wide and overhand) while extending the bar above his head. He keeps his elbows locked and shoulder blades squeezed together. He stands with his feet shoulder-width apart, his chest and buttocks out, and his knees slightly bent. He slowly descends by pushing his hips back and flexing at his hip and knee joints. He goes down until his thighs are parallel to the ground.

Coaching Point: Make sure the athlete does not let the bar travel past his shoulder blades.

#37: Squat Holds (Upper and Lower Legs)

Objective: To promote muscular strength, power, and endurance in order to increase leg speed

Equipment Needed: Physioball

Description: The athlete positions his feet shoulder-width apart. He lowers his body until his thighs are parallel to the ground and holds this position for two seconds. In the down position, he drives his heels into the ground, keeping his abdominals and glutes as tight as possible. This exercise can also be done against a wall, with a physioball behind the athlete's back.

Coaching Point: If the exercise becomes too difficult, have the athlete stand up and reposition himself.

#38: Stiff-Leg Dead Lifts (Hamstrings)

Objective: To promote muscular strength, power, and endurance in order to increase leg speed

Equipment Needed: Barbell with weight plates, step platform

Description: The athlete stands elevated on a platform with his back straight and his knees slightly bent. The barbell is placed just in front of the feet. The athlete bends over and grips the barbell with his hands shoulder-width apart. Once the barbell is secure, the athlete straightens up, keeping his legs stiff and his arms locked straight. He holds the weight for a count of eight and then lowers the barbell to the floor. He repeats for a prescribed number of repetitions.

Coaching Points:

- Make sure the athlete wears a belt and keeps his back straight.
- Have the athlete start this drill using a light weight.

#39: Hip Flexor Squats (Hip Flexors)

Objective: To promote muscular strength, power, and endurance in order to increase leg speed

Equipment Needed: Bench

Description: The athlete places his right leg on a bench behind him with his left foot firmly on the ground. He lowers his hips until his left thigh is parallel to the ground. He rises up after a prescribed number of repetitions and repeats the exercise with his opposite leg.

Coaching Point: In the down position, make sure the athlete is driving his heels into the ground, keeping his abdominals and glutes tight.

#40: Dumbbell Lunges (Upper and Lower Legs)

Objective: To promote muscular strength, power, and endurance in order to increase leg speed

Equipment Needed: Dumbbells

Description: With a dumbbell in each hand, the athlete strides out with his left or right leg so that his lead knee is at 90 degrees and his back knee is slightly bent. He lowers his body until his lead leg thigh is parallel to the ground while his back leg should be bent at the knee and almost on the ground. He rises up to the starting position by pushing his lead foot into the ground and maintaining a tight torso throughout the movement.

Coaching Points:

- Make sure the athlete's lead knee does not extend over his toes and he is keeping his chest up.
- In the down position, his trail leg should be two to three inches off the floor but never touching the ground.

#41: Box Step (Upper and Lower Legs)

Objective: To promote muscular strength, power, and endurance in order to increase leg speed

Equipment Needed: Step platform, dumbbells

Description: The athlete stands upright with his feet shoulder-width apart and a dumbbell in each hand. He steps forward up onto a step platform with his right leg and then drives his left leg up so that his thigh is parallel to the floor. He lowers his left leg back to the floor first and then brings down the right leg. He then repeats to the opposite side.

Coaching Point: Have the athlete focus on driving his leg up as high as possible to improve his range of motion.

#42: Leg Extensions (Quadriceps)

Objective: To promote muscular strength, power, and endurance in order to increase leg speed

Equipment Needed: Leg extension and curl machine

Description: The athlete sits on a leg extension and curl machine with his back straight, gripping the handlebars. He places his feet underneath the bar of the machine. He raises the bar by extending his legs as far as he can. He slowly lowers his legs down toward the starting position.

Coaching Points:

- A slow, controlled movement works best.
- To isolate one quadricep, leg extensions can be performed with one leg. Note: Less weight should be used for single-leg extensions.

#43: Leg Curls (Hamstrings)

Objective: To promote muscular strength, power, and endurance in order to increase leg speed

Equipment Needed: Leg extension and curl machine

Description: The athlete lies face down on a leg extension and curl machine, keeping his back straight. He places his feet underneath the bar and raises the bar with his feet by curling his legs as far as he can. He slowly lowers his legs down toward the starting position.

Coaching Points:

- A slow, controlled movement works best.
- To isolate one hamstring, leg curls can be performed with one leg. Note: Less weight should be used for single-leg extensions.

#44: Standing Calf Raises (Calves)

Objective: To promote muscular strength, power, and endurance in order to increase leg speed

Equipment Needed: Standing calf raise machine or step platform

Description: The athlete stands with his shoulders under a standing calf raise machine or on a step platform with his toes elevated and his heels hanging off the edge of the platform. He keeps his back straight and stands up on his toes as high as he can. He holds this position briefly before slowly returning to the starting position.

Coaching Point: Make sure the athlete raises and lowers his heels as high and as low as possible to help train his calves through the entire range of motion.

BALANCE AND FLEXIBILITY TRAINING

#45: Ball Leg Curl (Physioball)

Objective: To build strong core power

Equipment Needed: Physioball, floor mat

Description: The athlete places his feet on top of a physioball. He keeps his upper back on the floor and raises his hips and midsection off the ground. He drives his hips up and rolls the ball in toward his body while keeping his feet on the ball.

Coaching Point: Make sure the athlete's feet stay firmly on the ball while his hips move up and back before he curls the ball toward his body.

#46: Single Ball Leg Curl (Physioball)

Objective: To keep the core muscle group conditioned, which builds strong core power

Equipment Needed: Physioball, floor mat

Description: The athlete places one foot on top of a physioball with the other foot straight up in the air. He keeps his upper back on the floor and raises his hips and midsection off the ground. He drives his hips up and rolls the ball in toward his body while keeping his foot on the ball.

Coaching Point: Make sure the athlete's foot stays firmly on the ball while his hips move up and back before he curls the ball toward his body.

#47: Ball Hip Extension (Physioball)

Objective: To keep the core muscle group conditioned, which builds strong core power

Equipment Needed: Physioball, floor mat

Description: The athlete places his feet flat on top of a physioball. He lies on his back with his legs at a 90-degree angle and drives his hips up. He lowers his body to the starting position and repeats.

Coaching Point: Make sure the athlete keeps his feet firmly on the ball, which should remain close to his body.

#48: Single Hip Extension (Physioball)

Objective: To keep the core muscle group conditioned, which builds strong core power

Equipment Needed: Physioball, floor mat

Description: The athlete lies on his back with one leg at a 90-degree angle and the other leg firmly on a physioball. He drives his hips up and then lowers his body to the starting position. He repeats the stretch with the opposite leg.

Coaching Point: Make sure the athlete keeps his foot firmly on the ball, which should remain close to his body.

#49: Bridges (Physioball)

Objective: To keep the core muscle group conditioned, which builds strong core power

Equipment Needed: Physioball, floor mat

Description: The athlete puts his upper back on a physioball with his knees bent and his feet flat on the floor. He keeps his hands out at his side for balance and extends one leg back to the starting position. He repeats the same movement with the other leg.

Coaching Point: Make sure the athlete keeps his core and glutes tight when extending his leg.

#50: Long Jump (Plyometrics)

Objective: To increase leg speed

Equipment Needed: Rubber floor or nonskid surface

Description: The athlete stands with his feet parallel and shoulder-width apart. He swings his arms back while bending his knees and hips. He then swings his arms up and forward in an explosive movement. In midair, he raises his knees up to his body. He should land with his legs forward and bent at the knees to absorb the shock. He continues moving forward in a series of jumps.

Coaching Point: Remind the athlete to keep his core and glutes tight when extending his leg.

#51: Single-Leg Hops (Plyometrics)

Objective: To increase leg speed

Equipment Needed: Rubber floor or nonskid surface

Description: The athlete should stand on one leg and drive up and forward off his planted leg. He lands on the same foot and continues on the same leg. He uses his arms to balance himself and to carry his momentum forward. He then repeats with the opposite leg.

Coaching Point: Have the athlete begin this exercise slowly and increase his speed with each repetition.

#52: Alternate Leg Bound (Plyometrics)

Objective: To increase leg speed

Equipment Needed: Rubber floor or nonskid surface

Description: The athlete begins with a staggered stance and pushes off with his post (front) leg, driving his knee up to his chest. He extends outward with the driving foot to gain as much height as he can. He should use his arms for balance. He alternates landing and taking off with each leg.

Coaching Point: Have the athlete begin this exercise slowly and increase his speed with each repetition.

#53: Side Steps (Plyometrics)

Objective: To increase leg speed

Equipment Needed: Rubber floor or nonskid surface, sliding board (optional)

Description: The athlete stands with his knees bent and steps to the side as far as possible. He repeats with the opposite foot.

Coaching Points:

- If possible, use a sliding board for this exercise.
- Have the athlete begin this exercise slowly and increase his speed with each repetition.

#54: Knee Jumps (Plyometrics)

Objective: To increase leg speed

Equipment Needed: Rubber floor or nonskid surface

Description: The athlete stands with his arms out at chest height and his palms facing down. He squats down and drives his knees up as high as possible. He tries to touch his knees to his palms, tucking his feet under his body while jumping.

Coaching Point: Have the athlete begin this exercise slowly and increase his speed with each repetition.

#55: Side Jumps (Plyometrics)

Objective: To increase leg speed

Equipment Needed: Rubber floor or nonskid surface, Plyo Hurdles™ (varying heights from 2 to 12 inches)

Description: The athlete should jump up and over a set of Plyo Hurdles. He drives his knees up to his chest and swings his arms for momentum and balance.

Coaching Point: Have the athlete begin this exercise slowly and increase his speed with each repetition.

#56: Box Jumps (Plyometrics)

Objective: To increase leg speed

Equipment Needed: Rubber floor or nonskid surface, plyometric platforms (varying heights)

Description: The athlete should stand on a plyometric platform, drop down to the ground, and land with both knees bent and his feet together. He immediately drives his legs back up by jumping to the next platform or returning to the starting position. He should swing his arms up for momentum and balance.

Coaching Point: Have the athlete begin this exercise slowly and increase his speed with each repetition.

#57: Pool Dips (Plyometrics)

Objective: To increase leg speed

Equipment Needed: Rubber floor or nonskid surface, step platform or 45-pound weight

Description: The athlete stands on a step platform or a 45-pound weight. He balances on one leg and reaches the opposite leg out as if dipping his toe into a pool. He squats as low as possible in this position.

Coaching Point: Have the athlete begin this exercise slowly and increase his speed with each repetition.

Bonus: Superman (Pilates)

Objective: To strengthen the back muscles while elongating the spine; to reduce the risk of injury to the back

Equipment Needed: Pilates mat or nonskid surface

Description: The athlete lies on his stomach and extends his arms and legs out straight while lifting them simultaneously. He holds for four-second intervals (inhaling and exhaling for two counts each). The athlete should perform eight repetitions.

Coaching Point: Remind the athlete to work his abs but not to forget to focus on the opposing muscles in the back.

Bonus: Crisscross (Pilates)

Objective: To strengthen the oblique muscles (side abdominals) and lower abdominals

Equipment Needed: Pilates mat or nonskid surface

Description: The athlete lies on his back, with the lower back pressed to the ground and his knees up at about a 45-degree angle. He puts his hands behind his head with the fingers laced together, and lifts the shoulder blades off the floor without pulling on the neck. He slowly goes through a bicycle pedal motion, bringing the right knee in toward the chest and straightening the left leg out, while simultaneously turning the upper body to the right, taking the left elbow toward the right knee. He holds for one second and switches sides. He continues alternating sides in a pedaling motion for one to three sets of 12 to 16 reps. He should maintain even, relaxed breathing throughout the exercise.

Coaching Point: Make sure the athlete breathes out on each repetition.

Bonus: Leg Lift (Pilates)

Objective: To strengthen and lengthen the quadriceps (front of thighs); to work the lower abdominals; to help loosen the hip flexors

Equipment Needed: Pilates mat or nonskid surface, physioball or medicine ball

Description: Lying on his back, the athlete places one leg up on a physioball and the other leg on the ground. He slowly raises his leg up from the ground and slowly lowers it down. The athlete should perform 10 repetitions with each leg.

Coaching Point: Make sure the athlete breathes out on each repetition.

Bonus: Working to a Hundred (Pilates)

Objective: To strengthen all the muscles in the core area

Equipment Needed: Pilates mats or nonskid surface

Description: The athlete lies on his back with his legs bent up at a 90-degree angle. He lifts his shoulders off the floor and beats his arms 100 times against the side of his body.

Coaching Point: The athlete should work up to 100 repetitions in small increments to prevent any injury.

Bonus: Crunches (Abdominals)

Objective: To develop core strength; to increase power, endurance, balance, and flexibility

Equipment Needed: Pilates mat or nonskid surface

Description: The athlete lies on his back with his legs up and bent at a 90-degree angle. He places his hands across his chest and raises his chest toward his legs. The athlete should perform two sets of 25 repetitions.

Coaching Point: Make sure the athlete squeezes his stomach up toward his knees in a slow, controlled movement.

Bonus: Toe Touches (Abdominals)

Objective: To develop the quadriceps, glutes (buttocks), hip flexors, groin, and abdominals; to increase power, endurance, balance, and flexibility

Equipment Needed: Pilates mat or nonskid surface

Description: The athlete lies with his back on the floor and his legs straight up in the air. He reaches up and tries to touch his toes. The athlete should perform two sets of 25 repetitions.

Coaching Point: Make sure the athlete squeezes his stomach up toward his toes in a slow, controlled movement.

Bonus: Leg Raises (Abdominals)

Objective: To develop the quadriceps, glutes (buttocks), hip flexors, groin, and abdominals; to increase power, endurance, balance, and flexibility

Equipment Needed: Pilates mat or nonskid surface

Description: The athlete lies with his back flat on the floor. Keeping his back flat, he raises his legs up six inches off the ground and holds them for five seconds. He then raises both legs all the way up and back down to the original position without touching the ground. The athlete should perform two sets of 10 repetitions.

Coaching Point: Make sure the athlete raises and lowers his legs in a slow, controlled movement.

Bonus: Russian Twist (Lower Back/Abdominals)

Objective: To develop the lower back and abdominals; to increase power, endurance, balance, and flexibility

Equipment Needed: Pilates mat or nonskid surface, physioball, 25-pound plate

Description: The athlete should lie face up on a physioball with the ball resting on his upper back right at his shoulder blades. He grasps a 25-pound plate in his hands and raises his arms straight above his head. He rotates his torso to the left by rolling his entire body on the ball. He should now be facing to the left, with the ball on his left shoulder and left hip. The weight in his hands is still in the same position relative to his body. He brings the plate back to center, pauses, and then repeats to the right side. Center, left, center, right, center is one rep. The athlete should perform two sets of 15 repetitions.

Coaching Points:

- Make sure the athlete keeps his body stable when he rolls to the side.
- He should pause for two seconds when his body position returns to the center.

Bonus: Knee-Ups (Abdominals)

Objective: To develop the lower abdominals and hip flexors; to increase power, endurance, balance, and flexibility

Equipment Needed: Pilates mat or nonskid surface, physioball

Description: The athlete assumes a push-up position with his feet supported by a physioball and his hands placed on the floor shoulder-width apart. He brings his knees to his chest, keeping his feet on the ball, and then brings the ball back to a starting position. The athlete should perform two sets of 15 repetitions.

Coaching Point: To increase the difficulty of this drill, have the athlete move his toes down so that only the tips of his toes are on the ball.

Bonus: Dead Bug (Abdominals)

Objective: To develop the hip flexors, groin, and abdominals; to increase power, endurance, balance, and flexibility

Equipment Needed: Pilates mat or nonskid surface

Description: The athlete lies on his back with his right knee bent at a 90-degree angle and his right arm straight above his head. His left arm and hand is extended straight down over his thigh, with his heel being approximately 6 to 10 inches above the ground. He quickly switches positions so that his left knee is bent at a 90-degree angle and his left arm is straight above his head. His right arm and hand is extended straight down over his thigh, with his heel being approximately 6 to 10 inches above the ground. Left and then right is one rep. The athlete should perform two sets of 25 repetitions.

Coaching Point: Remind the athlete to keep his head off the ground at all times, tuck his chin to his chest, and keep his abdominals tight.

Bonus: Plate Touches (Abdominals)

Objective: To develop the mass of the quadriceps and abdominals; to increase power, endurance, balance, and flexibility

Equipment Needed: Pilates mat or nonskid surface

Description: The athlete sits on the floor with his legs in a *V* position, balancing on his butt. He holds a 10- to 25-pound plate and twists from side to side, touching the floor with the plate each time he twists to one side of his body. The athlete should perform two sets of 15 repetitions.

Coaching Point: Make sure the athlete is twisting from side to side as quickly as possible.

Bonus: Side Oblique Bridge (Abdominals)

Objective: To develop the oblique muscles of the abdomen; to increase power, endurance, balance, and flexibility

Equipment Needed: Pilates mat or nonskid surface

Description: The athlete lies on his side, then raises himself up onto his forearm, keeping his knees and feet on the ground. He drives his hips up and down, keeping his body straight. The athlete should perform two sets of 15 repetitions.

Coaching Point: Make sure the athlete has his hips pushed all the way forward.

Bonus: Seated Ball Twist (Abdominals)

Objective: To strengthen the abdominal muscles, particularly the rectus abdominis and external and internal obliques

Equipment Needed: Pilates mat or nonskid surface, small physioball

Description: The athlete sits on the floor with his knees bent and his legs eight inches off the ground. With a small physioball in his hands, he twists and touches the ground to his left side with the ball and then twists and touches the ground to his right side with the ball. The athlete should perform two sets of 15 repetitions.

Coaching Point: Make sure the athlete keeps his abdominals tight and does not let his feet touch the ground.

5

Technique Development for Punters

#58: Ball Drop (Basic)

Objective: To develop the skill of putting the football in the proper position for punting

Equipment Needed: Football

Description: The athlete stands with his punting foot pointing straight down the line. His hips, shoulders, and knees should be pointing straight ahead. Using the proper drop mechanics, he drops the football directly on the line. The ball should land flat and bounce straight back up, not forward or backward.

Coaching Point: Have punters work on this drill daily and during pre-game.

Front View

Rear View

#59: Leg Swing (Basic)

Objective: To improve the straight line kick and finish at the punter's head (i.e., right knee to right eye for a right-footed punter and left knee to left eye for a left-footed punter)

Equipment Needed: Football

Description: The punter positions himself the same as in #58: Ball Drop with his body pointing straight down the field and his punting leg on the line. He takes a step with his non-punting leg, and then mimics the punting motion straight down the line.

Coaching Points:

- Have the punter pick a point six feet in front of him to focus his eyes on as he swings through the spot.
- Make sure the punter's leg does not cross over the line.

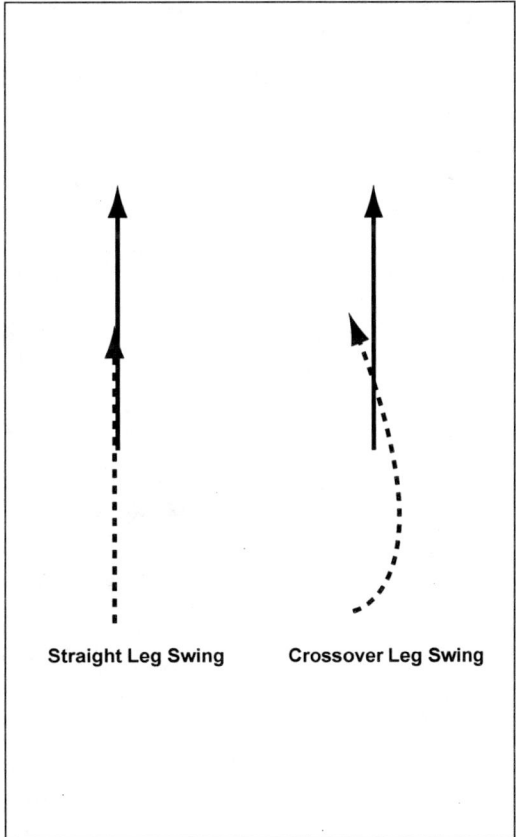

Straight Leg Swing   **Crossover Leg Swing**

#60: Line (Basic)

Objective: To emphasize correct ball placement, approach, leg swing, and follow-through

Equipment Needed: Football

Description:

- Ball placement: The punter starts with his punting foot on the line and extended. As the punter receives the ball, he should begin his approach. As he moves forward, the punter molds and places the ball in a direct line with his punting leg.
- Approach: The punter approaches the line of scrimmage in a straight line. As the punter approaches, his punting foot should step on the line, while his non-punting foot steps inches off center.

Coaching Points:

- Having the punter practice on a line will reinforce him doing all the mechanics in a straight line.
- If the punter is drilled to approach the line of scrimmage in a straight line during practice, he will also approach it in a straight line during games.
- Punters continually stress punting accuracy—as he punts the ball downfield, the line extended will become his target.

#61: Step (Basic)

Objective: To develop the punter's ability to remain compact through the punt and explode through the ball

Equipment Needed: Football

Description: The punter starts in the proper punting position. Someone tosses a football to him to simulate a snap (or he can bounce a ball off the ground to himself). Once the punter receives the football, he takes his step and swings his leg without punting the football. He lets the ball drop to the side of the swing. The punter practices the two-step and the three-step method using this drill. The punter must learn how to use each method in game situations.

Coaching Points:

- Make sure the punter's total operation is less than four yards.
- Stand behind the punter or work the drill on a line to assure straightness of form toward the target to maintain the punter's power zone.
- Emphasize having the punter develop a rhythm and smoothness in stepping and approaching the football.

#62: Towel (Advanced)

Objective: To prevent the punter from covering too much ground with his steps; to make sure the punter is contacting the football behind the block point

Equipment Needed: Football, two rolled towels

Description: A rolled towel is placed behind the punter's heel after he has assured his punting stance. Another rolled towel is placed four yards directly in front of the punter. The punter takes his steps and must make contact or punt the football behind or directly above the towel (four-yard mark).

Coaching Points:

- This drill is a great way to teach the proper stepping patterns for the three-step or two-step punt.
- To work on the two-step punt, shorten the distance of the front towel to three yards.

#63: Catch and Adjust the Ball (Advanced)

Objective: To improve catching skills; to shorten release time

Equipment Needed: Football

Description: Two partners stand 10 yards away from each other in good punting stances. Using one football, they toss it underhanded to each other, simulating a snap. Each partner should catch the football, rotate the laces so they face upward, and raise the football to the drop position as quickly as possible. The football may be held with an overhand, side, or underhand grip.

Coaching Point: To further improve the punter's catching skills, have the partners intermittently toss bad snaps during the drill.

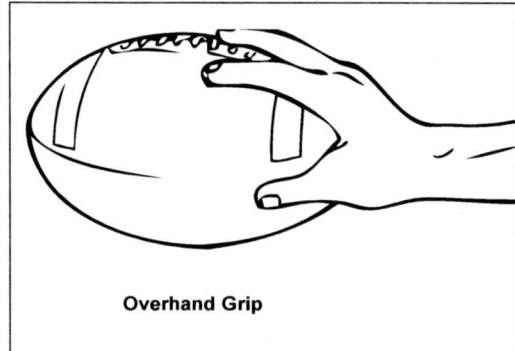

Overhand Grip

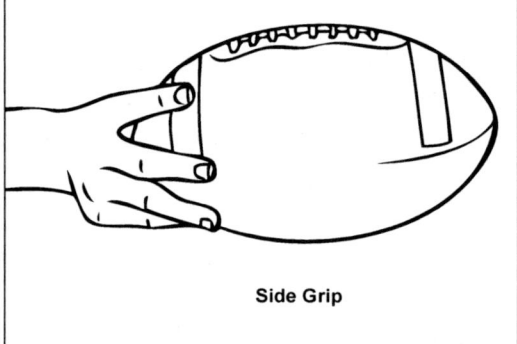

Side Grip

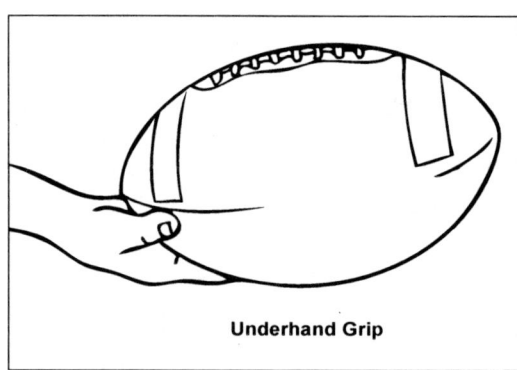

Underhand Grip

#64: Pressure Cooker (Advanced)

Objective: To develop the ability of the punter to maintain a smooth, controlled punting motion while under pressure

Equipment Needed: Football, agile bags

Description: Set up three agile bags to form a barrier around the punter, as shown in the diagram. The punter aligns inside the agile bags at a normal punting distance. Four rushers are positioned across the line of scrimmage from the center. On the center's long snap, one rusher takes off toward the punter. The punter catches the ball and begins his punting motion. The rusher uses the proper technique to block the kick, staying outside the agile bags.

Coaching Points:

- You can declare one side an overload and have the kicker punt the ball away from the pressure.
- The two inside players or two outside players can rush at the same time to provide more pressure.

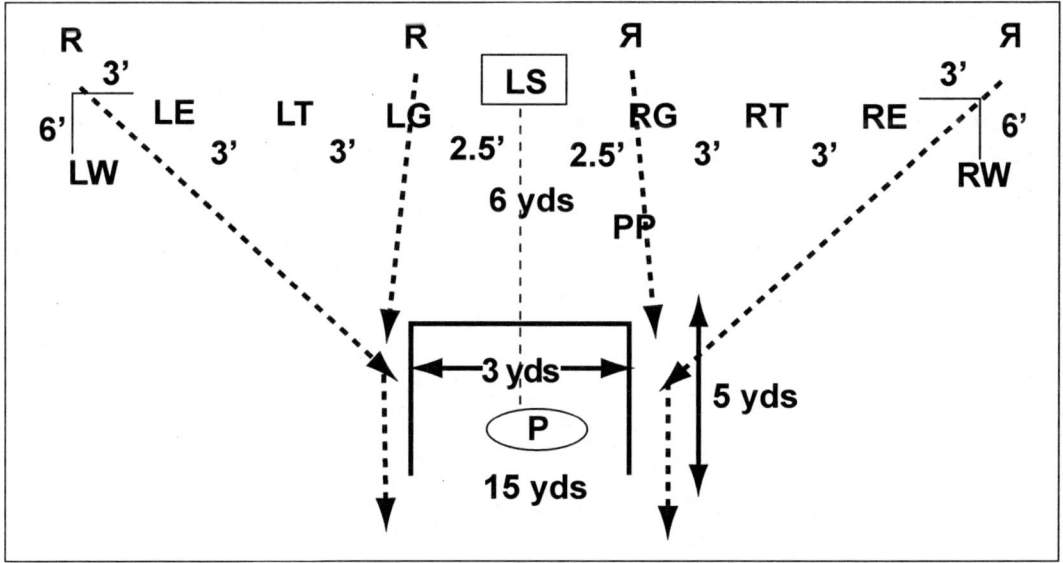

Bonus: Partners Catch (Advanced)

Objective: To develop the punter's skill of making good, flat contact with the foot and the football; to develop the punter's ability to control the direction of the football, which is essential in coffin corner punting

Equipment Needed: Football

Description: The punter stands 35 to 40 yards away from a partner. The punter takes one step, drops the football, and punts it to his partner, keeping the football flat and snapping the leg quickly through the football directly to the partner.

Coaching Point: Have the punter point his toe as much as possible toward his partner and quickly snap the leg through the football.

Bonus: Hang Time (Advanced)

Objective: To develop the proper technique for keeping the ball in the air longer (pooch kick)

Equipment Needed: Football, a tall object such as a stadium light pole, a tree, or a telephone pole (anything in the 100 feet high range)

Description: The athlete stands 20 yards away from the tall object and, using his normal punting technique, punts the football over (or as high as) the object. The only adjustment the punter makes is to hold the football longer before punting so that the contact with the ball is higher from the ground.

Coaching Point: Observe from the side if the punter should be making contact with the ball higher in his leg swing.

6

Skill Development for Man Protection Scheme and Coverage Punting Team

#65: Man Protection vs. Three Alignments (Individual)

Objective: To teach the proper stance and spacing while developing the techniques to block a man on the player's inside shoulder, head-up, and on the player's outside shoulder

Equipment Needed: Football

Description: Punt rushers are aligned on the blocker's inside shoulder, head-up, or on the blocker's outside shoulder. The blocker aligns properly—his toe is off the center's heel, his inside foot is up, his hands are in position to strike, and his eyes are on the target. On the snap of the ball, the rusher advances and the blocker uses proper footwork and hand contact to stop the rusher. If the rusher is on the inside shoulder, the blocker steps laterally to the inside, bringing the second step laterally with the first, and strikes the rusher with hand jams. If the rusher is head-up, then the blocker takes a quick up-down step with his inside foot and moves accordingly with his feet before striking the rusher. This timing step works well with stacked rushers. If the rusher is aligned to the outside shoulder (away from the football), then the blocker quick sets on the rusher. Jams are performed with the heel of the palms, thumbs up, using a short, strong, and quick punch of the arms.

Coaching Points:

- The blocker must be in a head-up position when the block is made.
- The blocker's shoulders must be square to the line of scrimmage at all times.
- Maintaining balance for proper release is a must for the punt protectors.

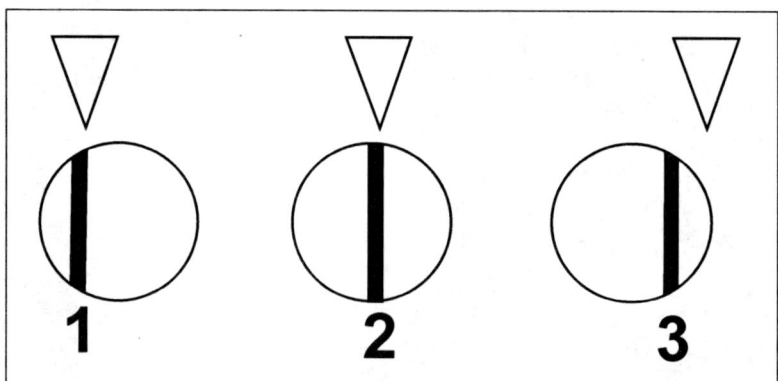

#66: Sink Technique (Group)

Objective: To improve the wing's ability to sink

Equipment Needed: Fire hose, football

Description: Align three rushers—two on a wing and one on a tight end (Diagram A). The rushers should align with proper spacing from the center. On the snap of the ball, the rushers get off and attempt to block the kick. The sink begins by the wing backpedaling and turning his butt slightly to the block point. The first two backpedal steps should be long and fast, then shorter and slower as the wing gets near the block point. The wing must maintain the track to the block point (X), jamming the defender without moving off the track. The tight end executes his technique according to the rusher's alignment (inside shoulder, head-up, or outside shoulder).

Coaching Points:

- Make sure the rusher never stops moving back.
- The drill may also be run without a tight end, using only two rushers.
- Optional drills would be to have the two outside (or inside) rushers cross (Diagram B) or to have one rusher sprint to the punter while the other rusher stops (Diagram C). These punt pressure combinations aid in checking the speed of the sink and maintaining the proper line to the block point.

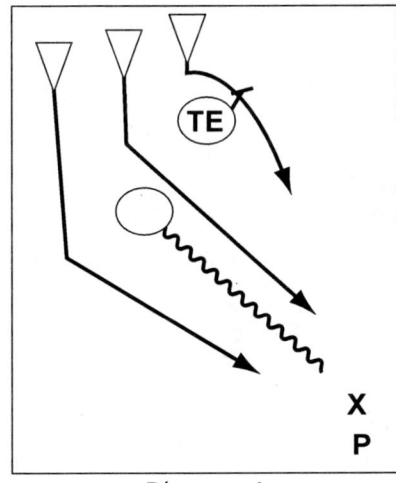

Diagram A

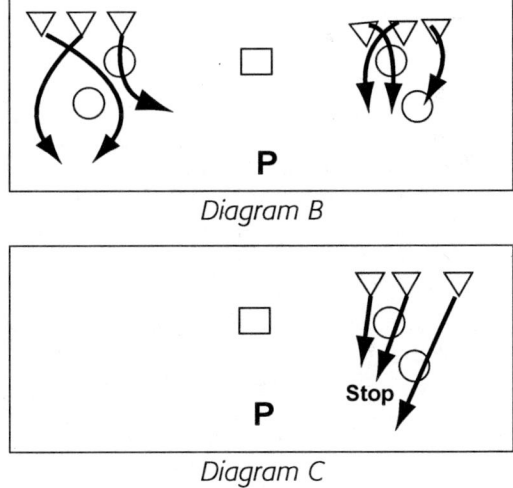

Diagram B

Diagram C

#67: Zone Protection vs. Stack and Twist (Group)

Objective: To develop the ability of the interior personnel in the punting team to block various stunting schemes

Equipment Needed: Football

Description: Align a guard, tackle, and tight end together in a group. Place two rushers in a stack either over the guard or over the tackle. Both inside stacks (Diagram A) and outside stacks (Diagram B) should be used. You will need to direct which way the stackers should rush. If the stack is inside, the guard, tackle, and tight end work toward the inside on the snap of the ball with lateral steps (shoulders square to the line of scrimmage) and pick the stack, always protecting the inside gap. If the stack is over the tackle, the guard will work toward his outside gap to pick the stack with the tackle. This stack is treated like a zone blocking scheme just as in pass protection on a pass rush twist.

Coaching Points:

- Players can be placed on the line of scrimmage and not in a stack to simulate a line twist (Diagram C).
- Players that are stacked can dance (move up and down) on the inside or outside of a gap to simulate different combinations that the opponent might be showing in their block pressure schemes (Diagrams D and E).

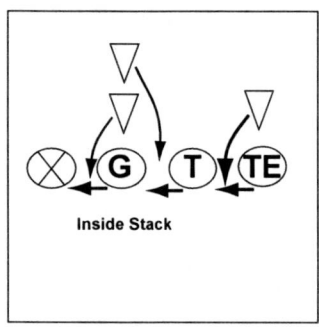

Inside Stack

Diagram A

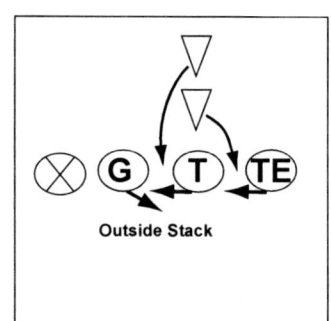

Outside Stack

Diagram B

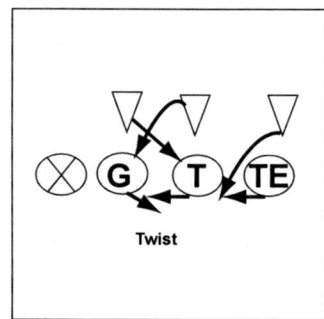

Twist

Diagram C

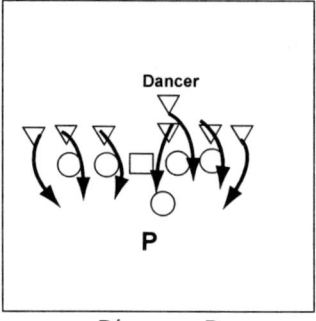

Diagram D

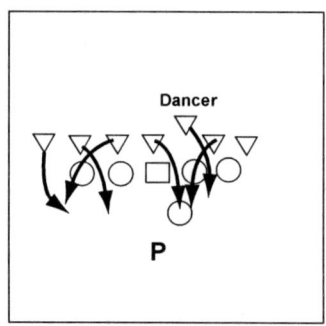

Diagram E

#68: Personal Protector Reads (Individual)

Objective: To train the personal protector to scan for the most dangerous man

Equipment Needed: Football

Description: Align three or four rushers ready to attack the punter. On the center's snap, the rushers attack the punter. The personal protector goes through his progression to establish the most dangerous man. The block progression is the A gap toward the kicker's leg, the wing toward the kicker's leg, and then the wing away from the kicker's leg.

Coaching Point: The personal protector should not back up to block. He must make his decision and meet the most dangerous rusher.

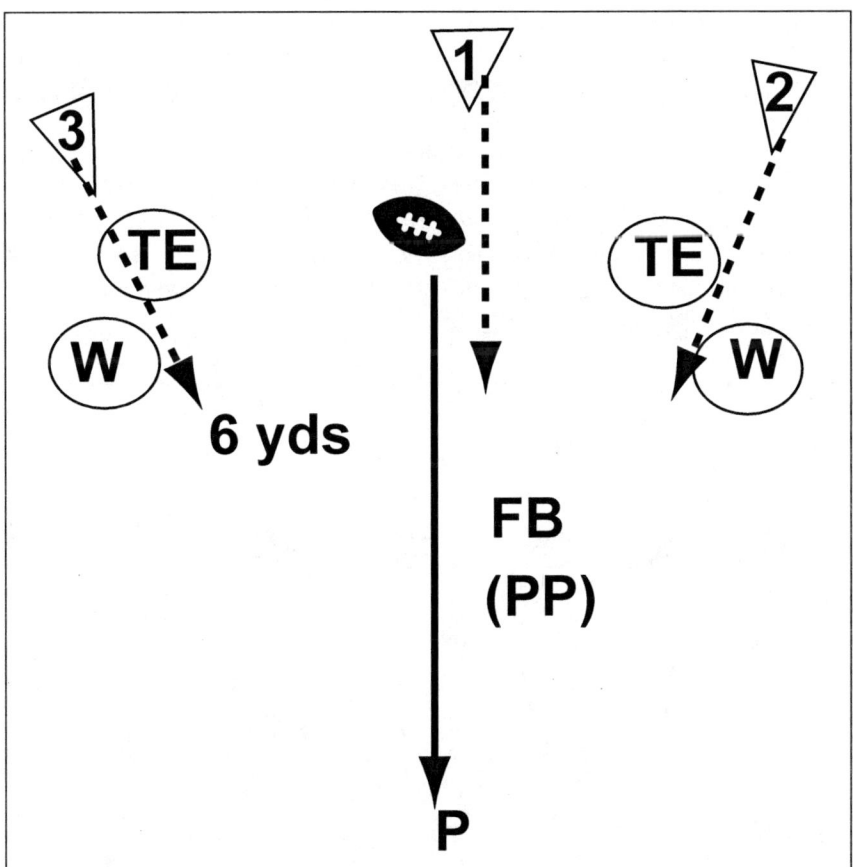

#69: Block Protection/Release/Landmark Development (Group/Team)

Objective: To practice executing the proper block protection, releasing using proper escapes, and getting to the coverage landmarks

Equipment Needed: Helmet markers, football, scout look cards (based on opponents' punt pressure schemes)

Description: Assemble a punt block or return unit and have them attack the punting team according to an opponent's schemes. The punt unit executes their blocking assignments and proper escapes (outside releases), heading toward the punted ball. (Coverage personnel need to listen for the punter's directional call and look at the returner to determine the location of the football.) For the first 10 yards (i.e., to the helmet markers), the players are working to be five yards from each other. As the coverage unit gets to the 10-yard mark, visual landmarks (numbers, hash marks, goal post) are used to maintain the coverage lanes. The drill continues until all players leverage the runner.

Coaching Point: Execute the drill from each hash mark and from the middle of the field. If you're a directional punting team, have the punter execute those punts also, which allows the coverage personnel to work on moving their coverage lane according to the punt placement. All the coverage players should imagine themselves being attached to a string to build a wall to stop the returner.

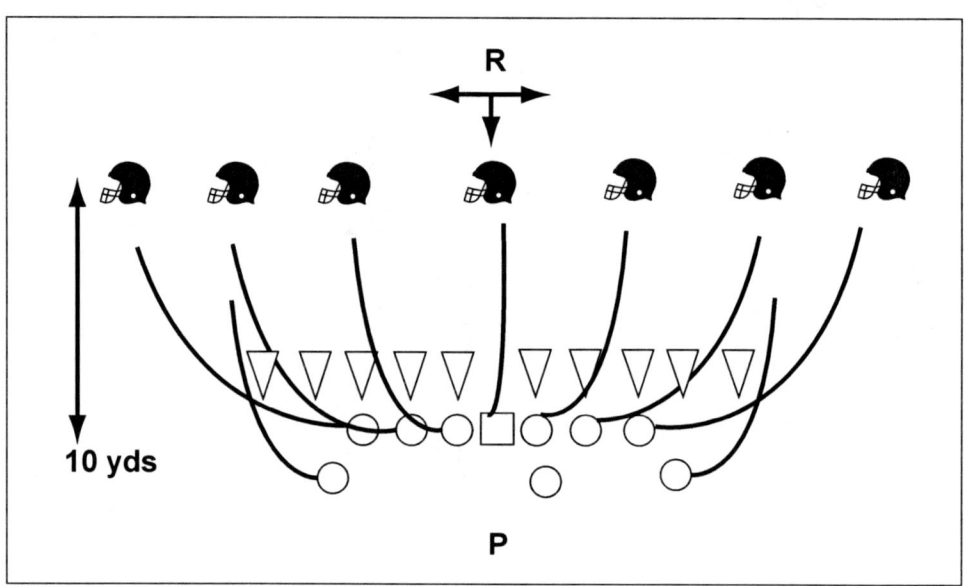

#70: Punt Coverage With Line Punt Blockers (Group/Team)

Objective: To develop the skills to escape from blockers while downfield covering the punt

Equipment Needed: Helmet markers, football

Description: The initial set-up and operation of this drill is the same as #69: Block Protection/Release/Landmark Development. The difference occurs when the 10-yard landmark is reached, where another set of players is waiting to pick up the punt coverage personnel on a trail and retrace. As explained in Chapter 3 (#27: Trail and #28: Retrace), the blockers will either block when the punt coverage player closes on the returner or retrace if the punt coverage player stops and goes over the top. The coverage player must maintain his leverage on the return and make a form tackle.

Coaching Point: Emphasize building a wall across the field, closing on the ballcarrier only when he has committed to a gap. The personal protector and the punter must be trailing the main coverage unit as safeties (12 to 15 yards behind).

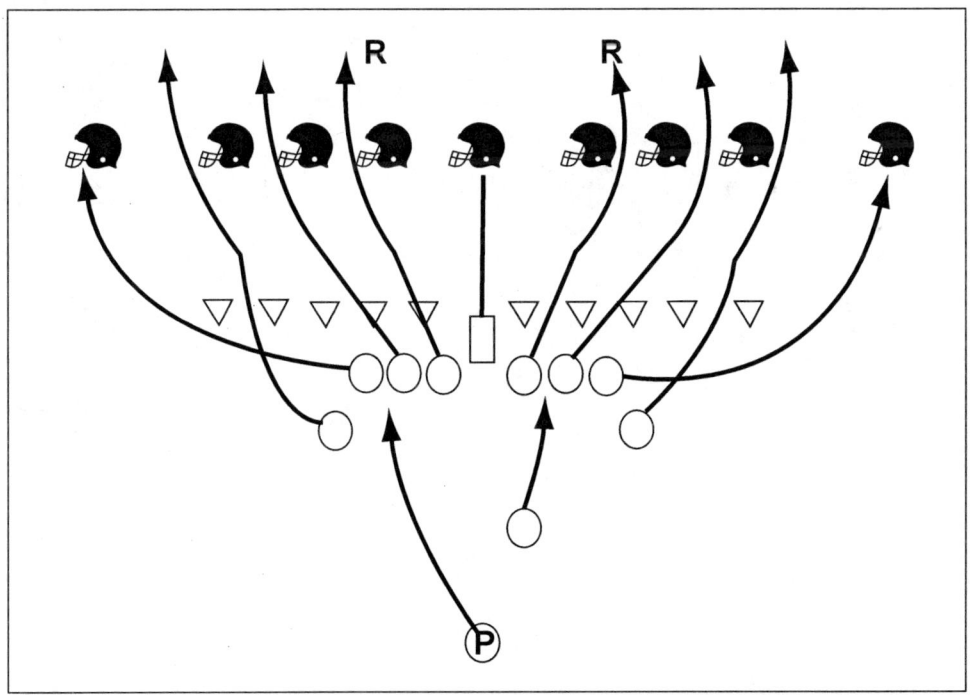

#71: Crossface Tackle (Individual)

Objective: To teach and practice avoiding the blocker and making a safe openfield tackle.

Equipment Needed: Five dots (used as landmarks for the blockers, returner, and defender), footballs

Description: The defender starts at a dot and sprints five yards. Have a coach point at a blocker to come at the defender. The defender gives the blocker a move (rip/swipe) and locates the return man. The return man goes left or right and the tackler must wrap up and drive him back.

Coaching Point: Emphasize the importance of using good technique on the blocker, maintaining a correct angle to the returner, and making a proper angle tackle.

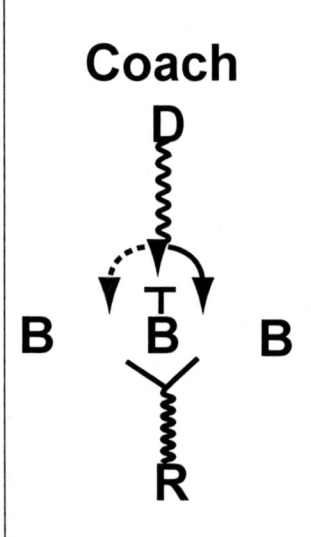 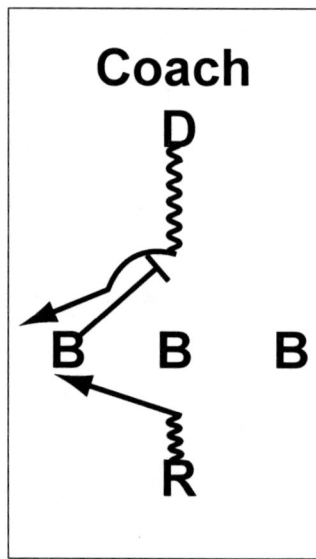 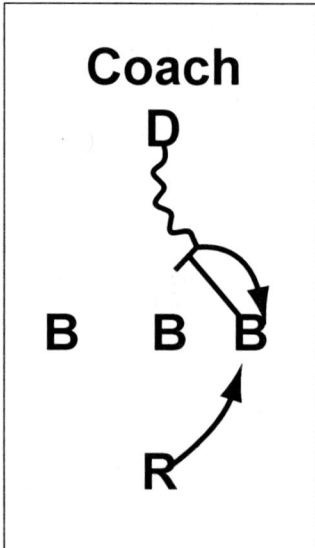

#72: Mirror Tackle (Individual)

Objective: To teach patience; to practice making an openfield tackle

Equipment Needed: Two cones, one dot, footballs

Description: Place two cones five yards from a dot, and align a tackler at one cone and a return man at the other. The tackler and the return man run toward the dot. When they reach it, they both break down and the return man shuffles right and left. On a coach's whistle, the tackler runs through the return man and makes the tackle.

Coaching Points:

- Make sure the athletes keep good football position when shuffling.
- Stress the importance of making a safe tackle.

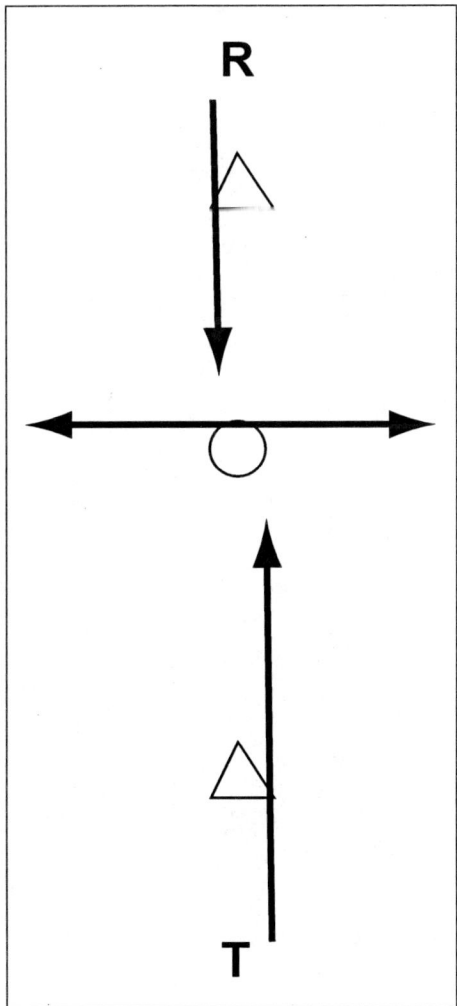

7

Technique Development for Kickers

#73: Dry Run (Basic)

Objective: To practice the entire kicking motion without kicking the football

Equipment Needed: None

Description: The athlete aligns, stands, approaches, and swings exactly as if he were kicking the football.

Coaching Points:

- This drill should be done during the last part of the warm-up routine, just after stretching to further prepare for kicking.
- Have the athlete do this drill along a straight line to check his form.

#74: Ball Contact (Basic)

Objective: To develop the ability to transfer and shift the swing momentum from the plant leg, through the football, and down the target line

Equipment Needed: Placekicking tee, football

Description: The kicker positions his plant foot next to the football exactly where it should be upon contact (six to eight inches to the side of the football with the instep even or just behind the seam of the football). The kicker places his kicking foot behind the football. He lifts all of his weight onto his kicking foot and then transfers his weight or rocks forward to his plant leg as he raises his kicking leg to kick the football. He pushes his body with his plant leg past the football upon contact to maximally transfer the momentum to the football (follows the target line). No steps will be taken to the football because his plant foot is already positioned.

Coaching Point: Have the athlete do this drill along a straight line to check his form.

#75: Plant and Drive (Basic)

Objective: To teach the proper leg stepping and positioning pattern, which is essential for good ball contact

Equipment Needed: Placekicking tee, football

Description: This drill is identical to #74: Ball Contact, except that one step with the plant leg is allowed. The athlete starts with his kicking foot to the back and side of the tee, staggered in front of the other foot. Leaning forward with his kicking foot in a good starting stance, he pushes off his kicking leg and steps with his plant leg and plants his foot. The kicker should keep his feet as close to the ground as possible and take compact steps, swinging his leg and kicking the football. He plants and drives down the target line, making sure not to hop in the air or lunge to the football.

Coaching Point: Have the athlete do this drill along a straight line to check the form.

The plant foot lands about a foot away from the tee at the midpoint.

The leg and ankle lock with the toes pointing down.

#76: Goalpost (Advanced)

Objective: To develop the proper height on kicks, which helps prevent kicks from being blocked at the line of scrimmage

Equipment Needed: Placekicking tee (or holder), football, goalpost

Description: The athlete should tee the football seven yards from the goalpost using a holder or tee. Using his normal extra point or field goal steps, he tries to kick the ball over the crossbar.

Coaching Points:

- Use caution because if the ball hits the crossbar, it will come back at a high rate of speed—be prepared.
- Make sure the kicker keeps his head down and follows through.

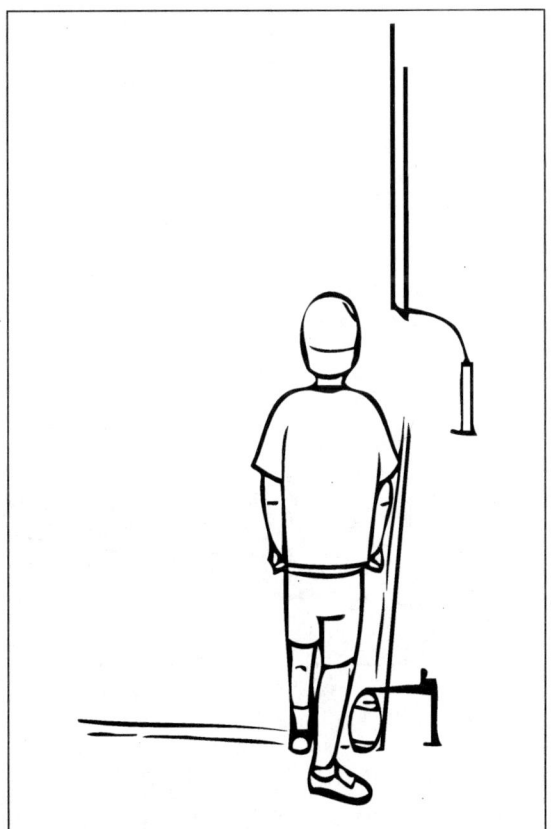

#77: Kicking at One Upright (Advanced)

Objective: To ascertain a kicker's command; to develop straightness of form, accuracy, and directional control

Equipment Needed: Placekicking tee (or holder), football, goalpost

Description: Have the athlete kick the football from the sideline at various distances (the goal line, five-yard line, 10-yard line, and 15-yard line) through the uprights using the proper technique. He should make good contact, push his body up through the football, and follow his target line.

Coaching Point: Make sure the kicker keeps his head down and follows through.

#78: Bad Hold (Advanced)

Objective: To develop mental toughness and confidence; to teach how to make the kick from a bad hold

Equipment Needed: Holder, football

Description: The athlete attempts to kick the football using his normal steps while the holder presents him with a variety of bad holds (e.g., the laces are facing the kicker, the football is on the end or one side of the block, the football is leaning too far back or forward, the football is let go before the kicker makes contact with the football, etc.).

Coaching Point: Make sure the kicker keeps his head down and follows through.

#79: Kicking H-O-R-S-E (Advanced)

Objective: To develop a competitive edge; to practice a variety of angles

Equipment Needed: Placekicking tee (or holder), footballs, goalpost

Description: Place footballs at different field positions and yard lines. Each kicker gets an opportunity to kick the ball and make a field goal. For every missed field goal, a letter is accumulated. If the word horse is spelled, the kicker is out of the competition.

Coaching Point: Utilize a center and a holder to simulate game-day situations.

8

Skill Development During the Specialist Period

#80: Money

Objective: To maximize the development of the various specialists during the designated specialist period, especially the punt pressure and extra point/field goal teams

Equipment Needed: Football

Description: The field is divided in half. On one side of the field are the punting and punt pressure teams and on the other side are the extra point and field goal teams. The pods drill (Chapter 3, #29) is executed by the scout punting team and the punt pressure unit. This drill is used to refine the execution of the punt return and block schemes in coordination with the returners. The punter works on punting out of the end zone, making sure to concentrate on the skills of not stepping backward out of the end zone, catching the football under pressure, and performing a one-step punt to get it off quickly. On the opposite end of the field are the short snappers, holders, and kickers, working on the extra point and short field goals, especially from the hash mark.

Coaching Points:

- For drill efficiency, determine the scout team personnel prior to the drill.
- A script should be developed that includes the punt returns and punt blocks, as well as the yard line, hashes, and fakes for the extra point/field goal units.
- Develop scout look cards so the punt and extra point/field goal block units can align and rush.

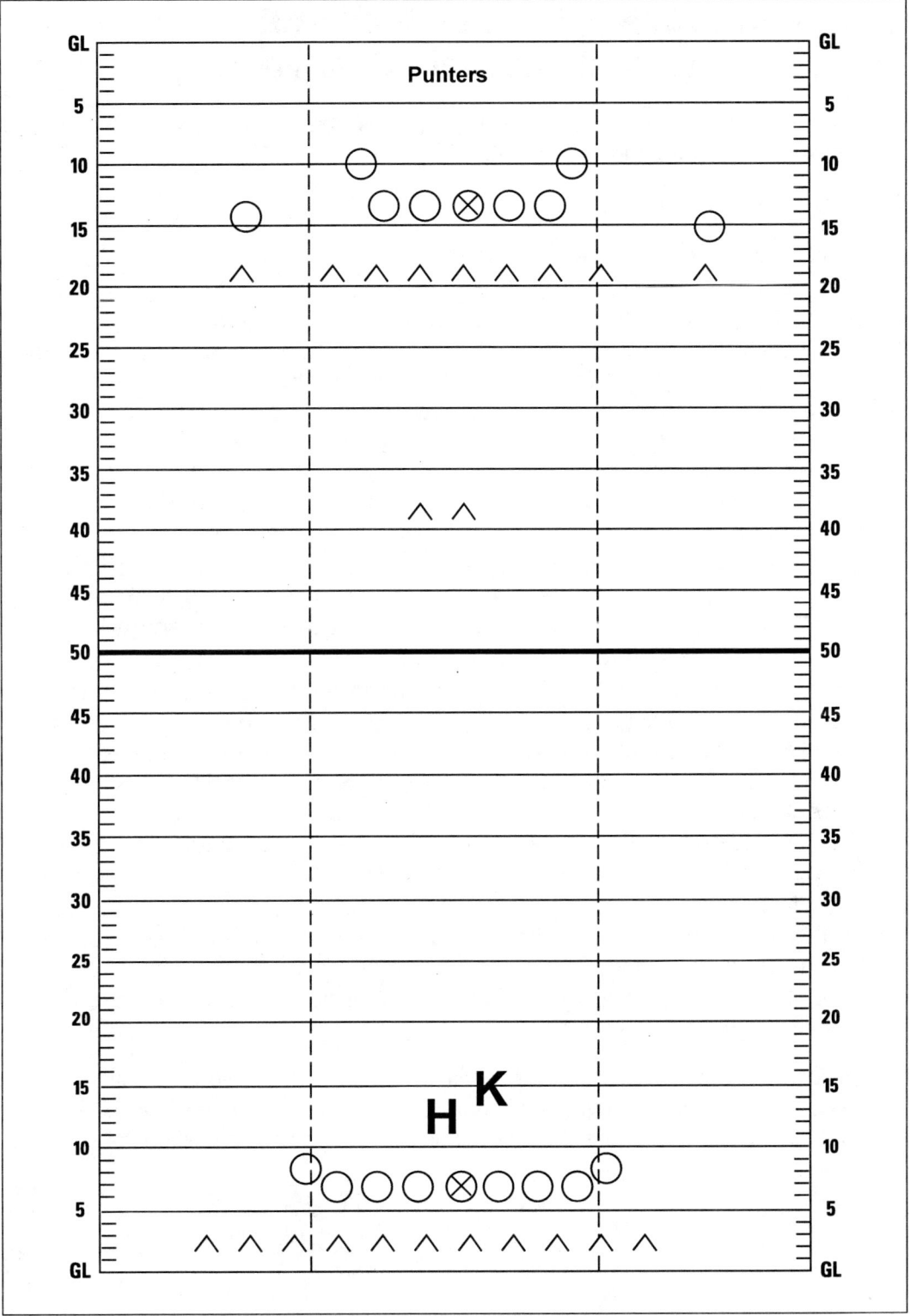

#81: Stinger/Swatter, Kickoff Returners, Extra Point/Field Goal Fakes

Objective: To maximize the skill development of the various specialists on punt coverage, kickoff return, and extra point/field goal units

Equipment Needed: Football

Description: The field is divided into four areas:
- On the right hash mark are the long snappers, punters, and gunners, with the returners downfield. The punters are working on their sky, directional, and coffin corner punts. The returners are working on fair catch mechanics, fair catch decoy mechanics, and communication if more than one returner is part of the scheme. When the ball is snapped, the gunner and swatters work on their techniques. The swatters can be single or double on the gunners. If the ball hits the ground, the gunners work on scoop and score. If it is a muff, they work on downing the football. If the returner catches it as they are closing in, the gunners work on tackling the returner (two-hand touch) or distracting them during the fair catch.
- On the left hash mark are the kickers and kickoff returners. The kickoff returners work on communication, reverses, lead blocking, and bursting upfield when the gap opens. The kicker works on directional kickoffs. Coverage players and kickoff return blockers can be added to sharpen their skills.
- On the opposite side of the field in the middle are the perimeter personnel for the extra point and field gold protection units (i.e., tight end and wings) along with the center, holder, and place kicker. On the opposite side of the protection unit are the extra point and field goal block units (edge rushers only). For five minutes, fakes and kicks are practiced. This time enables both units to work on scoring and defending against a fake when a block scheme is being utilized. Spend the next five minutes working on kicks where the only emphasis is on blocking the kick and protecting.
- To the left of the blocking/protecting operation are the first and second lines of kickoff return. Here, they are working on securing the football based on drive/squib/onside and pop-up kicks. The second line also works on catching the ball and pitching it back to the returner.

Coaching Point: Have more than one unit ready so that everyone designated as a specialist is working on improving their skills. Change the hash on the punt/kickoff and punt/kickoff return to maximize the effectiveness of each phase based on field position.

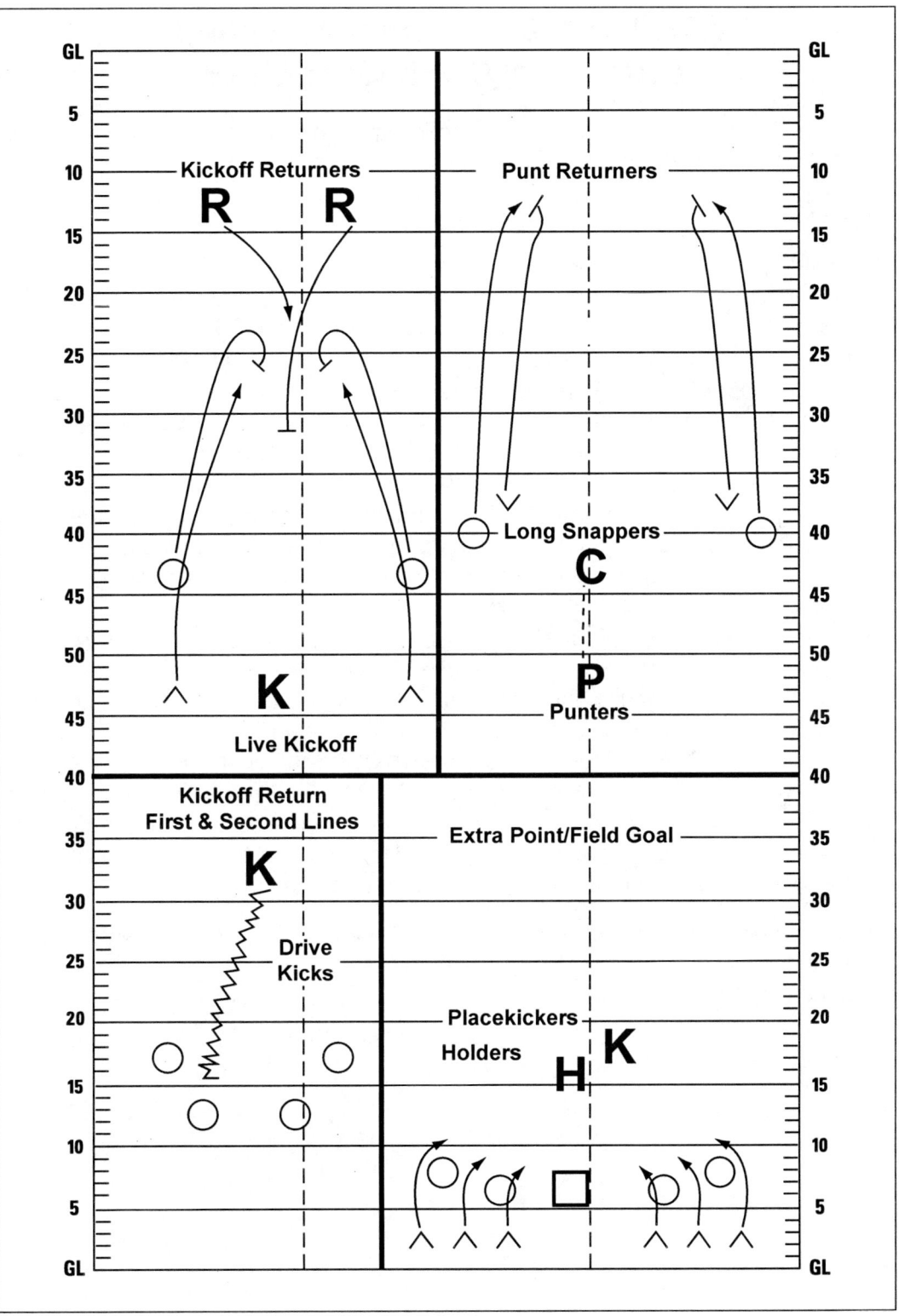

#82: Punt Return, Punt Coverage, Extra Point/Field Goal Block

Objective: To maximize the skill development of the various specialists on the punt return, punt coverage, extra point/field goal block units

Equipment Needed: Footballs

Description: The field is divided into five areas:
- On the left hash mark are the punters with long snappers and returners. Here, they are working either solo or in tandem. The 11-yard fair catch mechanics are also being practiced.
- On the opposite hash mark are the kickoff returners and kickoff personnel. The kicker is now kicking out of the end zone in order to practice both left and right directional kickoffs. Returners are working in tandem emphasizing communication, reverses, lead blocking, and bursting upfield when the gap opens.
- On the opposite side of the field in the middle are the extra point and field goal units (protection block perimeter). Spend the first five minutes with the emphasis on the extra point. Spend the next five minutes on the field goal, randomly moving the ball back to various hash marks.
- On the opposite side of the field on the left are the interior of the punt unit and gunners and swatters working on downing the football. A coach or another punter kicks the ball softly so that the football rolls. The punt coverage personnel chase the ball down in groups of two or three and use the proper techniques to pin the ball before entering the end zone. The punt team covers the punt in units (i.e., gunners, next two players inside, interior players) just like in the pods drill (Chapter 3, #29).
- On the opposite side of the field on the right are the extra point and field goal interior block specialists and protection unit. Here, each unit is working on perfecting their techniques. Get-off is emphasized for the block unit.

Coaching Point: Designating personnel in advance and posting assignments will preserve time and allow for more reps in which to enhance the development of fundamentals and schemes.

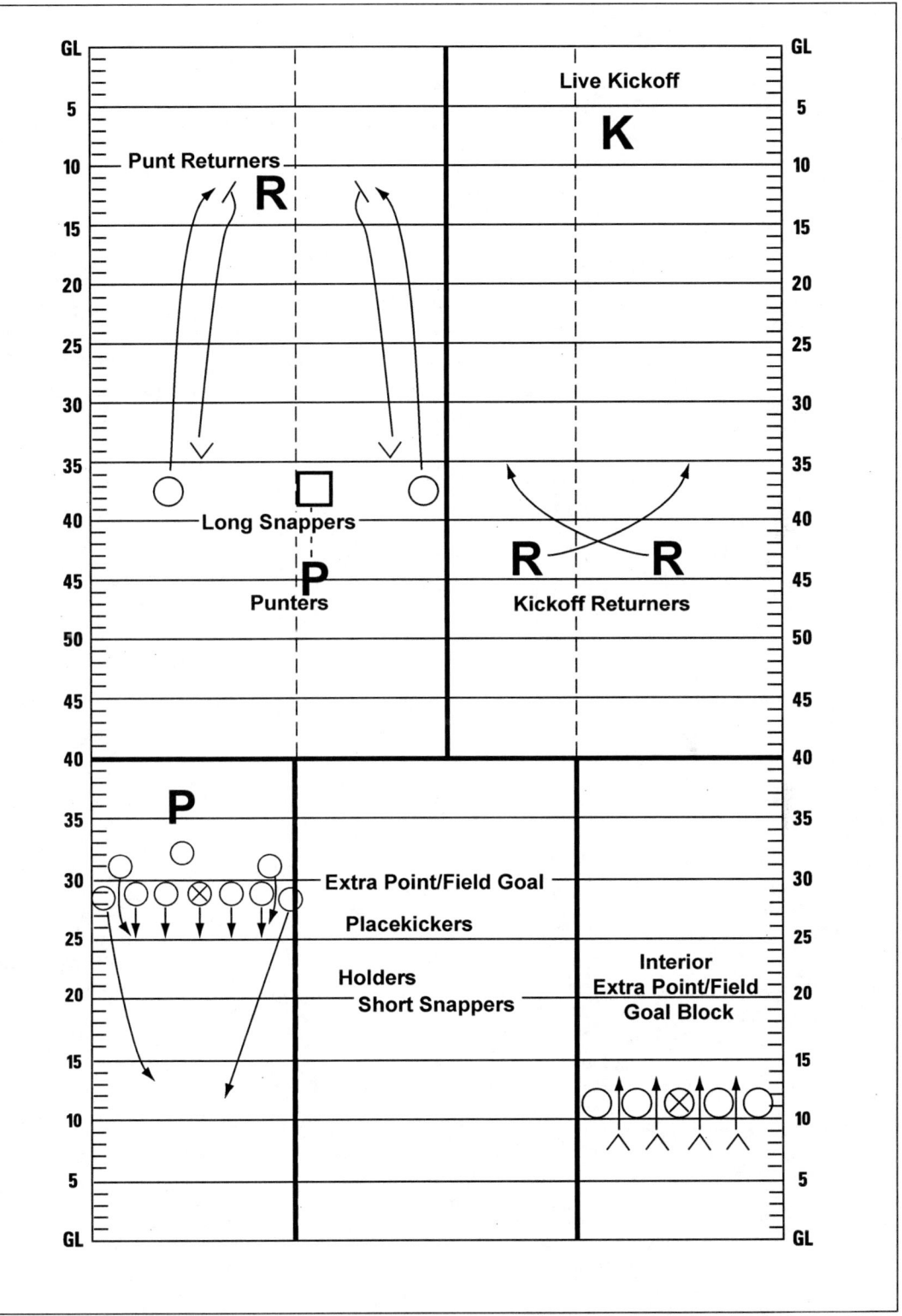

9

Skill Development for Blocking Extra Points and Field Goals

#83: Edge Rush Technique (Individual)

Objective: To teach players the proper way to block a PAT or field goal from the edge

Equipment Needed: Football, cones

Description: Set up a snapper and a corner rush player. Place a cone approximately one yard behind where the tight end would be aligned. Have a coach with a football stand where a holder would normally be. The snapper simulates a snap and the corner rush player rushes to the area in front of the kicking point (i.e., "the spot"). As the rusher comes off the corner around the cone, the coach tosses the ball forward and the rusher lays out and blocks the ball.

Coaching Point: The rusher should come off the corner as close as possible to the cone. The rusher should dip his shoulder, bend, push off his outside foot, point the toe of his inside foot, rip with his inside arm at the cone, and accelerate to "the spot" in front of the kicker, then dive with the shoulders and numbers facing the kicker in order to block the ball.

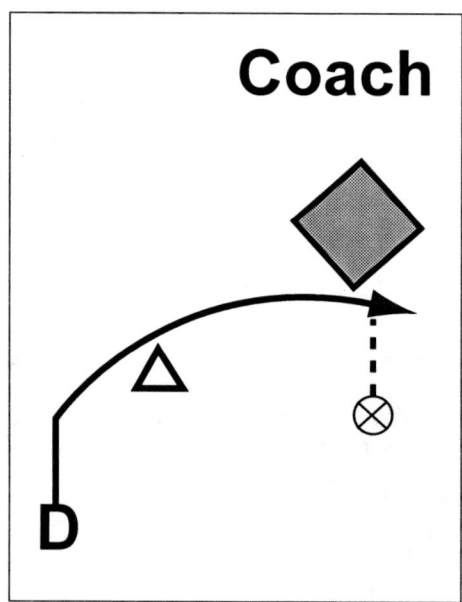

#84: Rush Off the Corner (Group)

Objective: To develop the skills of edge rushers in order to create 2-on-1 situations when blocking PATs and field goals

Equipment Needed: Football

Description: Assemble the outside personnel for extra point and field goal protection (tight end and wing) and block units (pull-down player and two rushers). On the snap of the ball, the pull-down player rips through the tight end gap or pulls the tight end forward, opening up the jump-through gap. The inside rusher aligns slightly cocked to the inside shoulder of the wing, and takes his first step upfield with his outside foot across the line of scrimmage. On his second step, he jumps over and steps through the gap between the tight end and the wing. He uses his hands to aid him on the shoulders of the tight end and the wing. He steps and flattens out to "the spot" (four-and-a-half yards behind the center). If the wing closes down hard on him, the inside rusher must occupy the wing, creating a clear course for the outside rusher. One man can not be allowed to block two rushers. The outside rusher aligns slightly cocked to the wing with his outside foot back. He aligns wide enough to get a good, close angle to "the spot." He takes his first step with his outside foot across the line of scrimmage. He takes his second step with his inside foot and with his third step, he drives off his outside foot to the inside, adjusting his course. With his fourth step, he takes off and lays out with his arms extended and his eyes open, moving his hands to the ball.

Coaching Point: Rushers must watch the ball and get a good initial takeoff, giving an all-out effort throughout every block attempt.

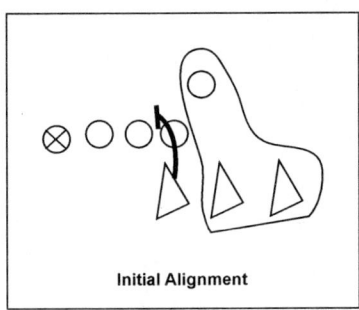

Initial Alignment

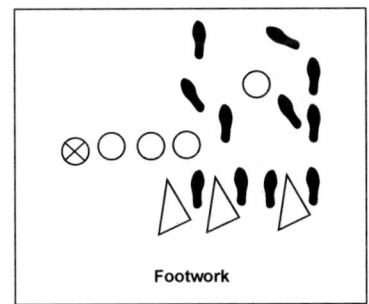

Footwork

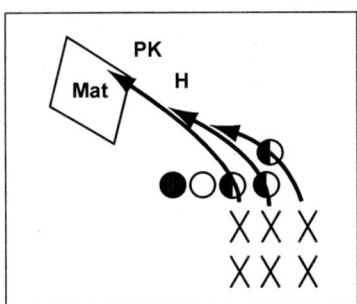

#85: Jump Block (Individual)

Objective: To develop the technique of blocking a placement kick up the middle or with a low trajectory kick

Equipment Needed: Footballs

Description: As a ball is being snapped, a jumper walks up a few steps to the line of scrimmage. Then, as the ball is being kicked, he jumps to block the kick.

Coaching Point: Steps and timing by the jumper are the keys to a successful block.

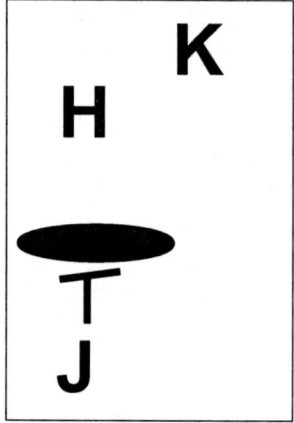

#86: Push (Group)

Objective: To teach the interior rush players how to knock back the line of scrimmage and get their hands up to block extra point and field goal attempts

Equipment Needed: Football

Description: Align interior linemen on the offensive line. Have the pushers work on driving their designated offensive linemen back using hand jams. The penetrator needs to work on getting skinny and firing through the gap, getting his hands up for the block.

Coaching Point: Rushers need to crowd the football and have great get-off explosion on the snap.

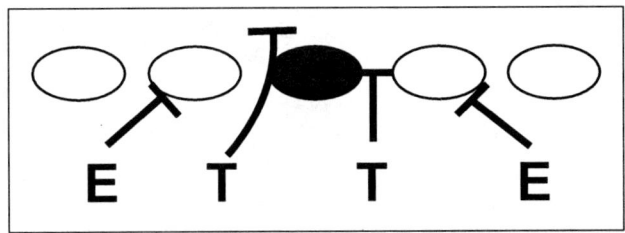

#87: Scoop and Score (Group)

Objective: To teach how to scoop and score on blocked kicks and how to contain on fakes

Equipment Needed: Football

Description: Players align with their assignments as the scoop and score players on the perimeter extra point/field goal unit (wing, tight end). The coach aligns where the kicker would be and flips the ball outside as if the ball had been blocked. The players scoop the ball up and run 10 yards, simulating scoring.

Coaching Point: The coach can add fakes to teach the block personnel to read on the run and stop a fake kick play.

10

Skill Development for Long and Short Snappers

#88: Warm-Up for Long and Short Snappers (Individual)

Objective: To improve the center's ability to explode the ball through the snap with his entire body

Equipment Needed: Football

Description:

- *Large arm circles:* The center extends his arms away from his body at shoulder height. He moves his arms like a windmill, using large circular movements (five times forward and five times backward).
- *Forward pass:* The center grips the ball like a quarterback and throws the ball overhand four times.
- *Underhand softball toss:* The center grips the football similar to a quarterback. He turns his hand under like he is snapping in a normal alignment. He swings his arm back like a softball pitcher. He accelerates his arm forward and releases the football.
- *Overhead snapping:* The center grips the football similar to a quarterback (Diagram A) and places a guide hand on the ball (Diagram B) while the ball is chest high. He takes the ball and rapidly places it over his head. The hands and ball are now inverted (upside down). His elbows and knees should be slightly bent and his feet should be slightly under his shoulders. Once the ball is overhead, the center slightly rotates the wrist of his throwing hand as if the ball and hand were on the ground in the normal centering position (Diagram C). Then, he accelerates his hands as if snapping underhand, and releases the ball, performing a complete snap motion from set-up to follow-through. His fingers must spin the ball out with his thumbs and fingers facing upward. As his arms are in motion, he should thrust his hips forward to create more power to snap.

Coaching Point: Make sure the centers are fully warmed up before executing long snaps.

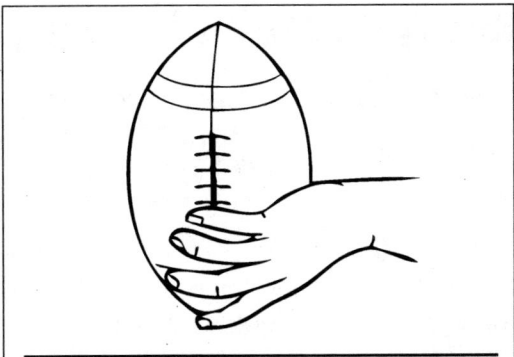

The throwing hand should be near the back of the ball, with the fingers spread.

Diagram A

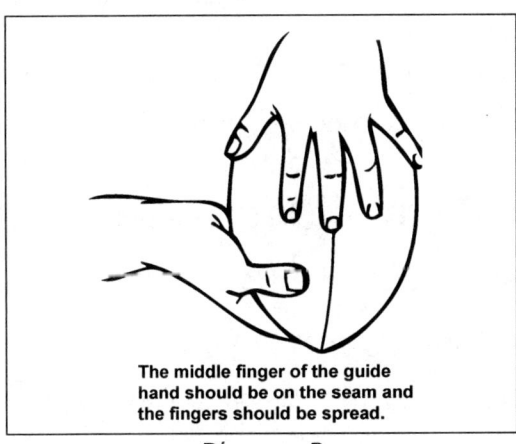

The middle finger of the guide hand should be on the seam and the fingers should be spread.

Diagram B

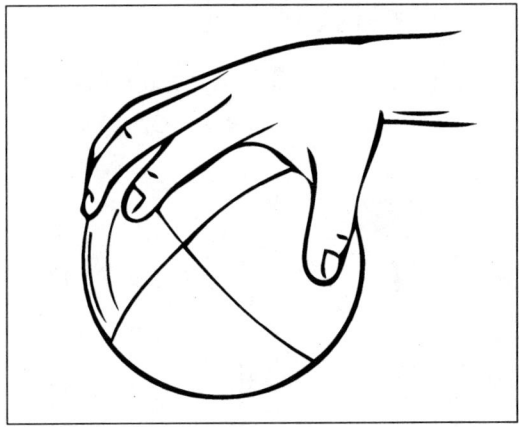

Diagram C

#89: Jog, Ready, Snap, and Cover (Individual)

Objective: To develop rhythm and smoothness in the center's punt procedure, from approaching the football to blocking and covering the kick

Equipment Needed: Football

Description: A football is placed on the field as if an umpire had just placed it ready for play. The center jogs to the football and sets his feet and hands properly. A defender aligns over or to the side of the center. The personal protector calls the cadence. The center snaps the ball to the punter and the center executes a block technique or releases to cover the football. If the defender is blocking for a return, the center needs to use various escape techniques (e.g., dip and rip, retrace feet) to cover the kick.

Coaching Points:

- The center must snap the ball with his fingers—not his palms.
- Options for this drill should include snapping with a wet ball and milking the clock.

#90: Tunnel (Individual/Group)

Objective: To improve the accuracy of the long snap

Equipment Needed: Football, agile bags, stand-up dummies

Description: Align the center with the punter at the normal punt distance. Surround the kicker's legs with three agile bags on the turf to simulate a box around the punter. On the front corners of the box, place two stand-up dummies. Have the center snap the ball to the punter between the two stand-up dummies.

Coaching Point: As the center's accuracy improves, the distance between the bags can be closed.

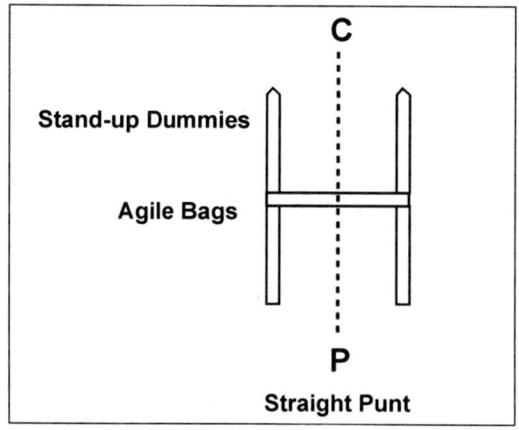

Straight Punt

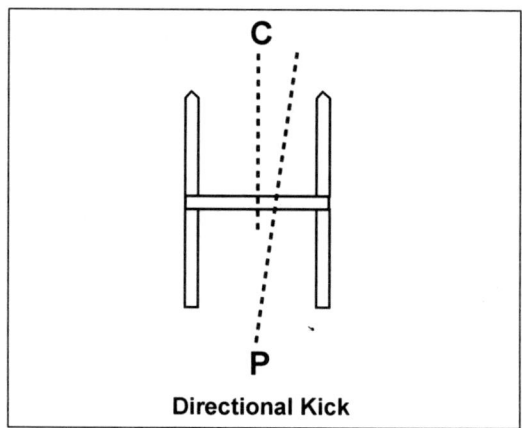

Directional Kick

11

Skill Development for Kickoff and Punt Returners

#91: Getting North and South (Individual)

Objective: To develop the returner's awareness of a defender coming toward him; to develop the returner's ability to catch the ball under pressure and make the defender miss the tackle

Equipment Needed: Cones

Description: Set up this drill according to the diagram. A coach starts the drill by throwing a ball to simulate a punt. The returner catches the ball using the proper mechanics (shoulders square to the line of scrimmage, elbows tight to the body), sets his eyes upfield, and locates the defender. Once the defender is sighted, the returner runs up the field towards the defender. The returner makes the defender miss the tackle and bursts upfield. The returner must stay inside the cones.

Coaching Points:

- The returner must *first* focus on catching the ball properly and *then* on setting his eyes on the defender to plan his escape move from the defender.
- As an option on this drill, the returner can work on administering a proper fair catch signal and performing a decoy fair catch.

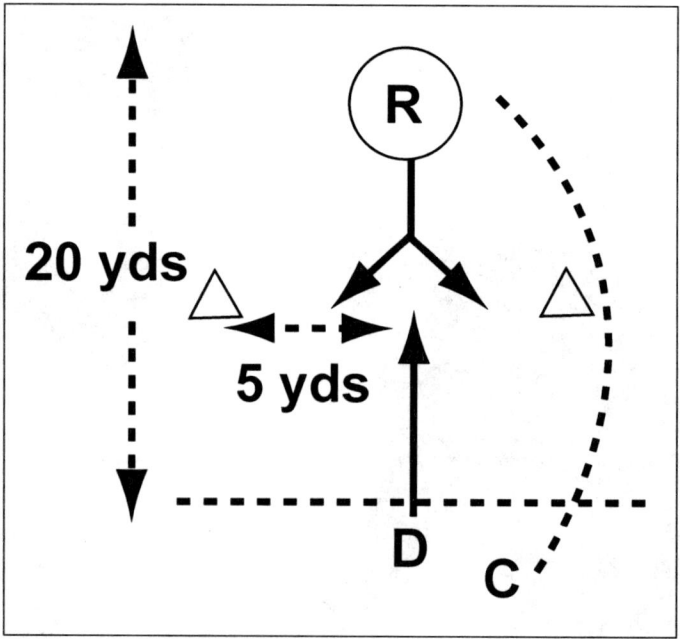

#92: Read and React (Individual)

Objective: To teach the returner to accelerate upfield and cut to the open hole

Equipment Needed: Barrels (plastic garbage cans), shields

Description: Set up the drill as shown in the diagram. The returner catches the ball from a coach or another player and accelerates toward the middle barrels. As the returner approaches, a coach holding a hard shield steps into one hole. The returner reads, reacts, and accelerates up to the open hole.

Coaching Points:

- Don't let the returner slow down.
- If the returner makes a poor read, the coach should use the shield and the returner should blast through the pad, using a stiff arm, lowered shoulder, or tight spin.

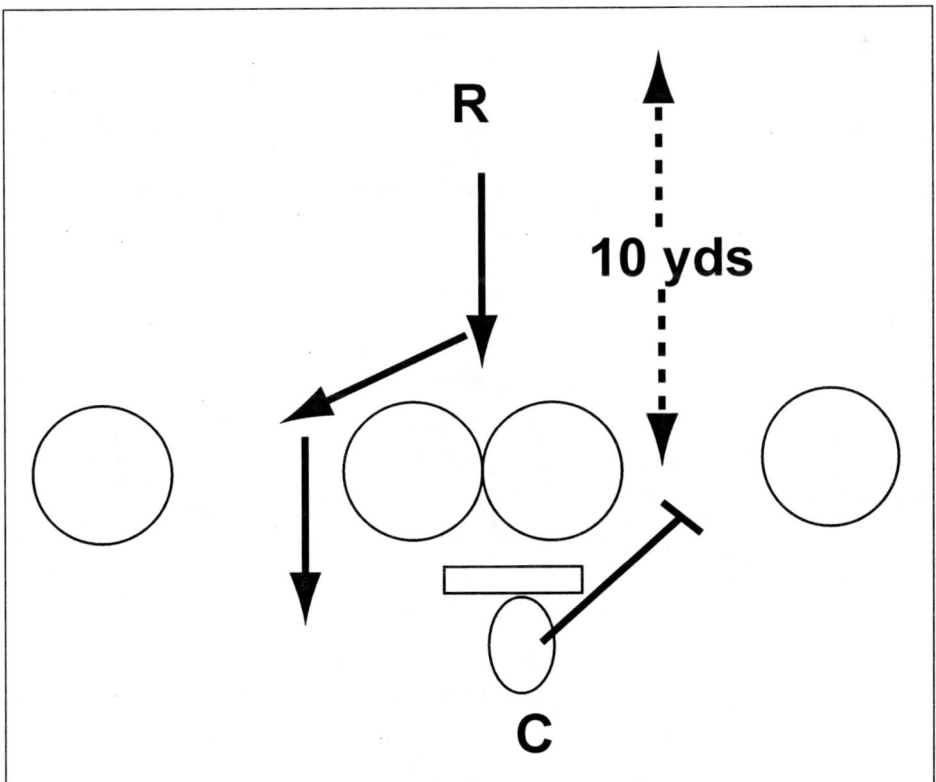

#93: Turnbacks—Locate the Ball (Individual)

Objective: To improve the ability of the returner to focus on the ball in flight and to read the spin of the ball

Equipment Needed: Football

Description: The returner stands with his back to the coach. The coach throws the ball to simulate a kick. When the ball is in flight, the returner turns around, locates the ball, and catches the ball using the proper technique.

Coaching Point: Utilize different ball rotations or a live kicker/punter to simulate game conditions.

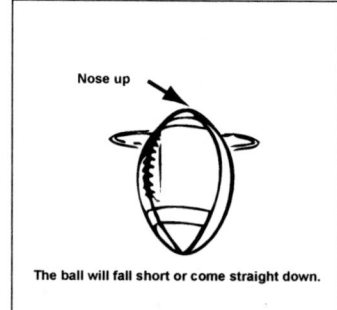

Nose up

The ball will fall short or come straight down.

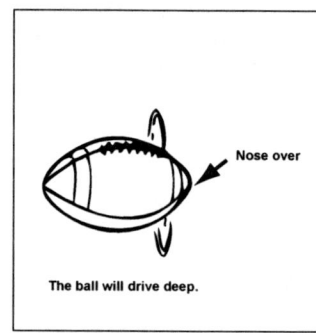

Nose over

The ball will drive deep.

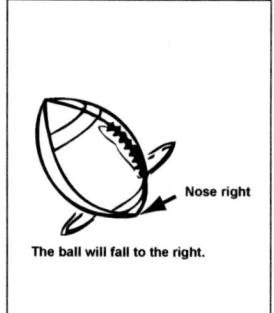

Nose right

The ball will fall to the right.

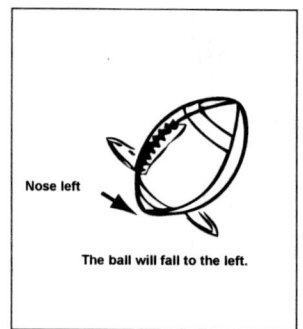

Nose left

The ball will fall to the left.

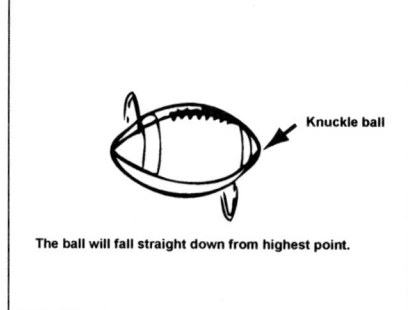

Knuckle ball

The ball will fall straight down from highest point.

#94: Dodgeball (Individual)

Objective: To improve the returner's ability to avoid tacklers while moving north/south upfield

Equipment Needed: Football, soccer balls, barrels, cones

Description: Set up the drill as shown in the diagram. The coach flips the ball to the returner, who fields the ball in flight. Once the ball is caught, the returner moves directly upfield to the first cone. As the returner moves up the field through the area outlined by the barrels, a player in a kneeling position (represented by a circle in the diagram) tosses a soccer ball at the returner, who maneuvers his body to avoid contact with the ball without breaking his momentum upfield. The returner can straight-arm the ball.

Coaching Points:

- Additional cones can be added for the returner to weave through as he runs upfield.
- Adding a second soccer ball thrower (as shown in the diagram) makes the drill more fun and it more closely simulates game conditions.

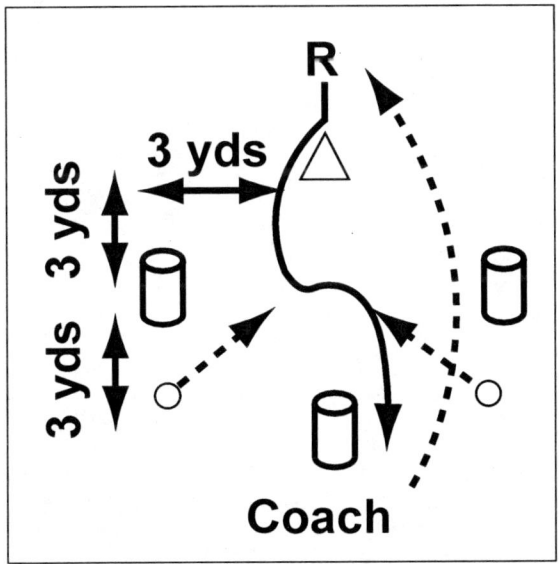

#95: Three-Returner Strip (Individual)

Objective: To emphasize the importance of ball security

Equipment Needed: Football

Description: Align three returners side by side about five to seven yards apart. A ball can be punted or a coach can throw a ball to one of the returners. As the ball is being caught by one returner, the other returners encompass the ballcarrier and go after the ball by stripping, ripping, or punching the ball out of the ballcarrier's hands as he moves upfield.

Coaching Point: The ball must be caught using the proper technique and secured immediately with five points (single hand) on the ball before moving upfield.

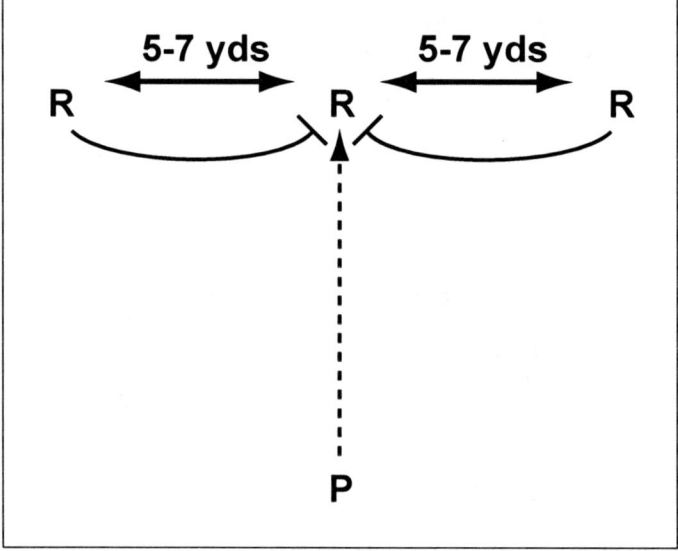

#96: Noodle Catching (Individual)

Objective: To improve the returner's ability to catch a football properly with his elbows tight to his body

Equipment Needed: Swim noodle, football

Description: Place a swim noodle under a returner's armpits and around his back. The returner uses arm pressure to squeeze the noodle as the ball is approaching in flight.

Coaching Points:

- The ball can be punted or flipped by the coach.
- The returner must maintain equal pressure with both arms.
- The noodle should barely protrude past the armpits.
- A rolled-up towel can be substituted for a swim noodle.

12

Skill Development for Stingers (Gunners) and Swatters (Defenders)

#97: Lock 'Em Up

Objective: To develop the ability of the defenders (swatters) to work as a 2-on-1 unit to control the opponent's forcers, totally removing them from covering punts

Equipment Needed: Football

Description: Align two swatters on each shoulder of a forcer (gunner) as diagrammed. The defenders will split the outside and inside legs on the forcer. They will outleverage him on both the outside and inside. When the forcer releases outside, the outside defender uses a bump-and-run technique, maintaining outside leverage. The inside defender remains on the hip of the outside defender and does not allow the forcer to split them or crossface. When the forcer releases inside, the inside defender uses a bump-and-run technique while the outside defender remains on the hip of the inside defender and does not allow the forcer to split them or crossface.

Coaching Point: Have the forcer, once he is downfield about 15 to 20 yards, cross over the blockers from his original path.

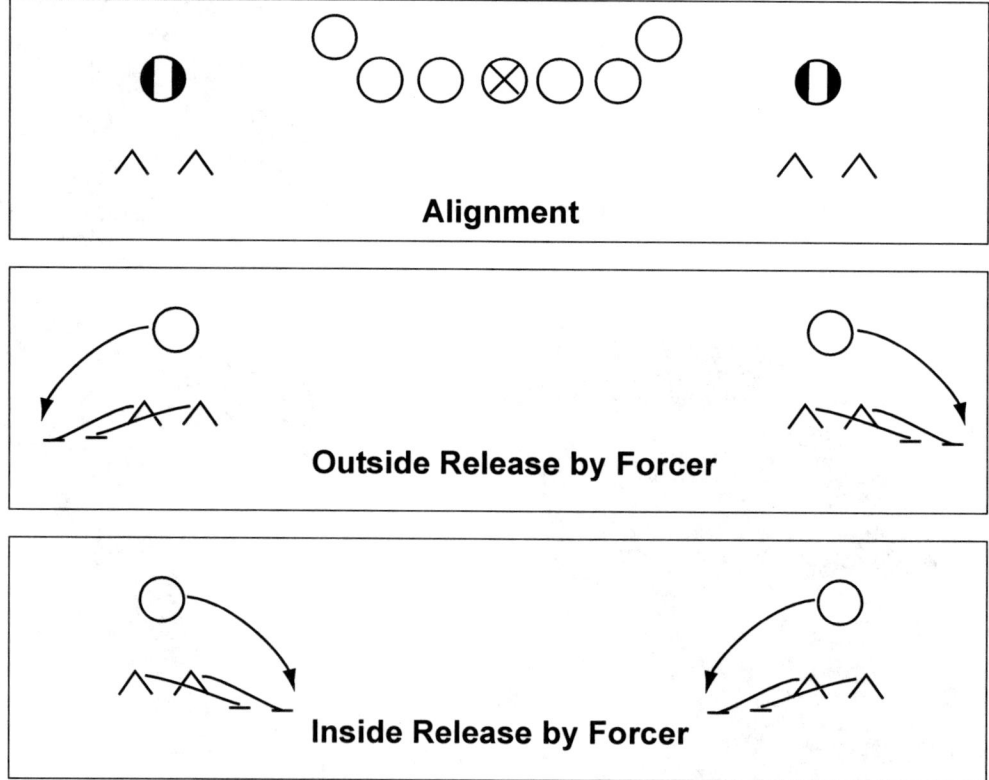

Alignment

Outside Release by Forcer

Inside Release by Forcer

#98: Stingers vs. Swatters (Group)

Objective: To improve the techniques of the forcers (gunners) and defenders (swatters) on the punt and punt return teams

Equipment Needed: Football

Description: Align the defender on the inside shoulder of the forcer. The defender must be parallel to the line of scrimmage. On the snap of the ball, the forcer takes off and utilizes an escape move such as a dip-and-rip technique, swim, or swipe in combination with foot fakes. The defender uses man (bump-and-run) techniques to ward off the coverage player.

Coaching Points:

- Forcers must concentrate on squeezing the returner while not making contact with him.
- The defenders must stay focused on each movement of the defender and retrace if the forcer changes directions.

#99: Fair Catch/Coverage (Group)

Objective: To improve the ability of the forcers to close in toward the returner and maintain coverage, without contacting the returner in a fair catch situation

Equipment Needed: Football

Description: Two pairs of forcers (gunners) and defenders (swatters) are aligned on opposite hash marks (as shown in the diagram). On the center's snap to the punter, the forcers take off toward the returner. The forcers must keep their eyes on the returner and gauge the proper approach to maintain leverage on the punt returner. The punt returner signals for a fair catch, working on the 11-yard rule.

Coaching Points:

- Increase the speed of the drill to full speed to simulate game conditions.
- As an option on this drill, the returner drops the ball, one forcer scoops and scores, and the other forcer blocks either the returner or the swatters who are attempting to tackle the scoop-and-score forcer.
- As another option on this drill, the returner signals a fair catch and moves away from the ball. The forcers (gunners) work together to down the football.

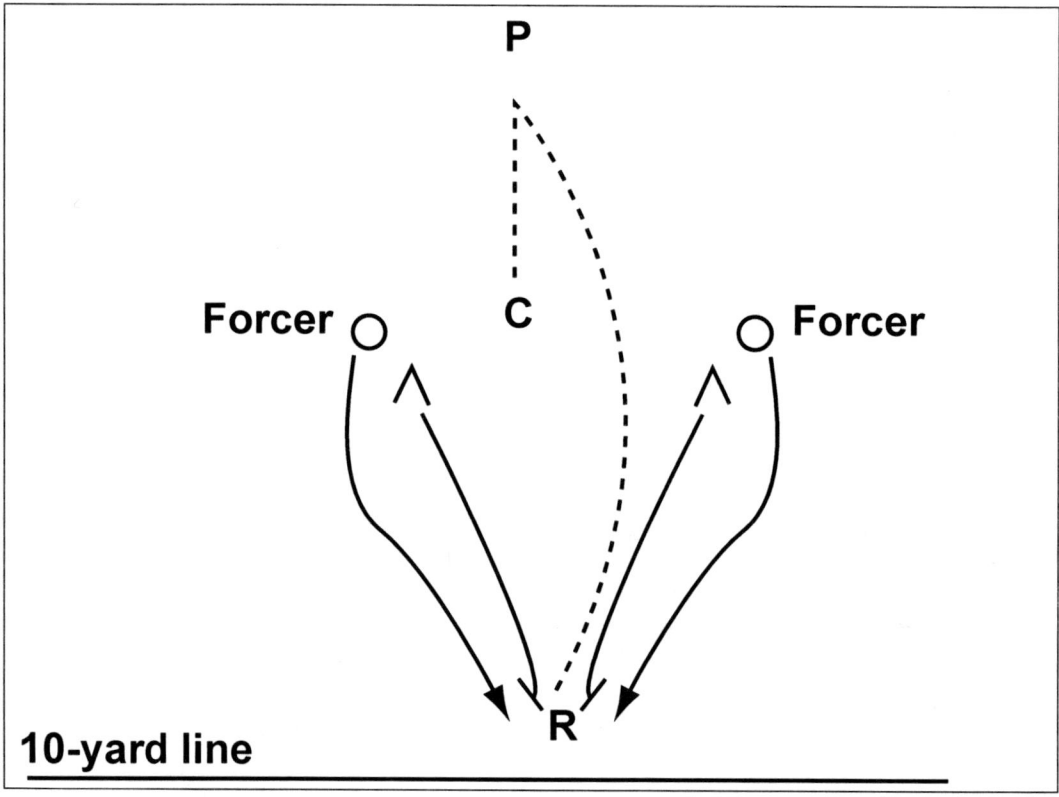

118

#100: Vicers (Stingers vs. Swatters) (Group)

Objective: To improve the ability of the stingers (gunners) to release during a punt return; to improve the ability of the swatters (defenders) to prevent the release during a punt return

Equipment Needed: Cones, football

Description: Place two cones five yards apart. Have the players align in the middle of the cones. On the go command, the players shuffle in a mirror-type action. The gunner is trying to gain an advantage to get a release. On the release command, the gunners use dip-and-rip footwork, knocking hands down to get past the swatter. The swatter uses a bump-and-run technique to maintain his blocking position. Continue the drill for five yards upfield.

Coaching Points:

- Players must maintain line of scrimmage resolution throughout the beginning portion of this drill.
- The drill can continue until the swatter can overtake the gunner.

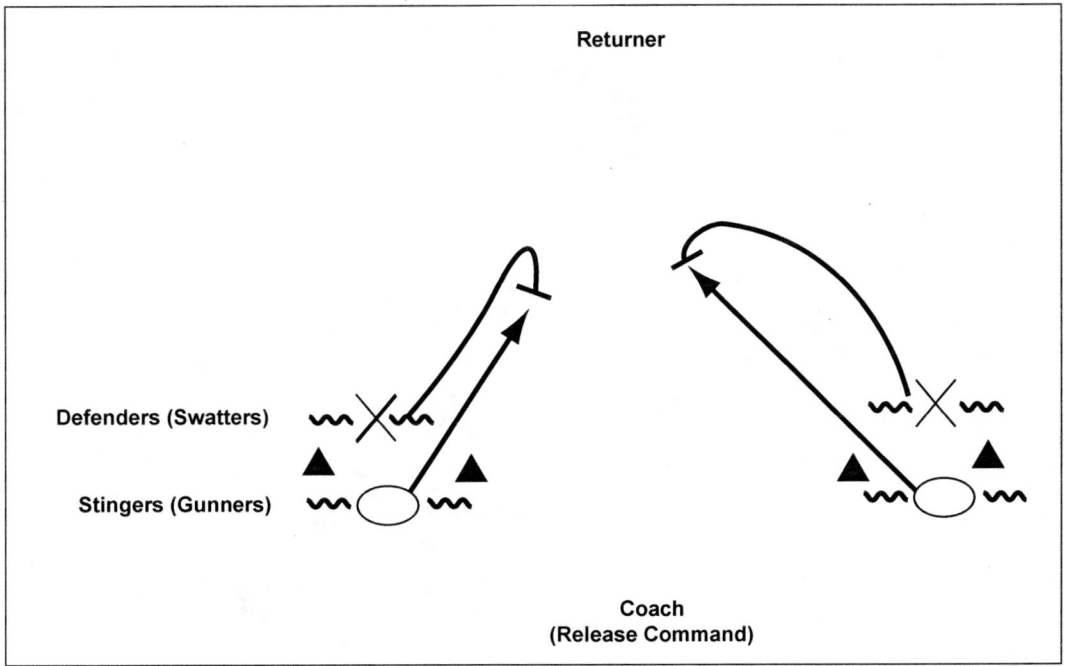

#101: Continuous Retrace (Group)

Objective: To improve the footwork of the defender (swatter) when covering a forcer (gunner)

Equipment Needed: Football

Description: One forcer (gunner) and one defender (swatter) align in a bump-and-run technique. On the go command, the forcer takes off downfield with an inside or outside release. The swatter defends the initial release, stemming the gunner according to the scheme. The gunner, once overtaken by the swatter, changes direction, and the drill continues.

Coaching Point: Run this drill at three-quarter speed until the swatter's retrace techniques have been perfected, and then increase to full speed to simulate game conditions.

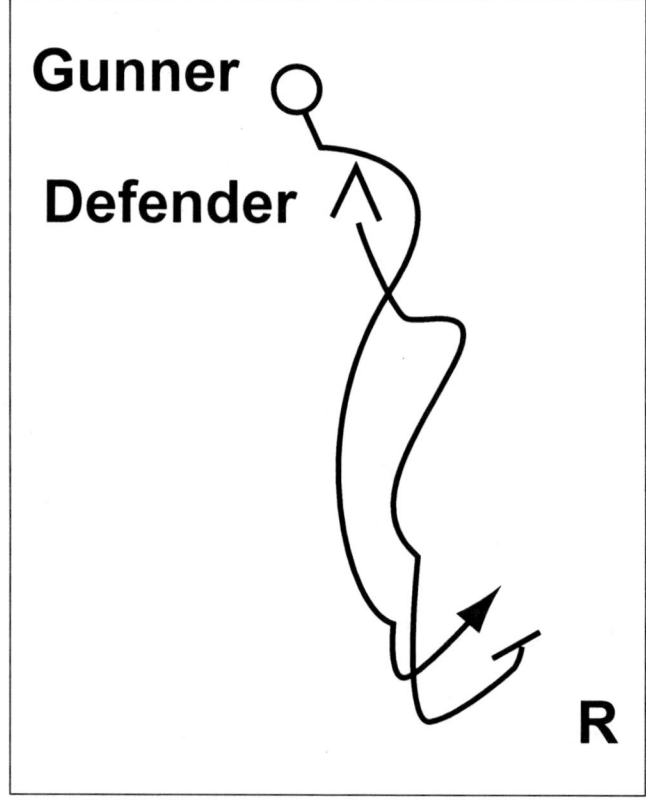

About the Author

Mike Cieri is a coaching veteran of 33 college seasons and 39 seasons overall, including high school. Cieri is the special teams coordinator and defensive line coach for the 10th winningest Division III football program, Montclair State University. Since 2003, Cieri's special teams have made six touchdowns from kickoff and punt returns, produced 56 blocked kicks (26 punt, 30 extra point/field goal), and scored a total of 60 points from those efforts. The Red Hawks have ranked number one in kickoff returns and/or punt returns for six out of the last eight years in the very strong New Jersey Athletic Conference. In 2010, Cieri's punt return units ranked in the top three nationally among Division III teams, with the nation's second-best punt returner. The Red Hawks' punting and kicking units have ranked number one over the past three seasons in net punting and field goal percentages and ranked second in kickoff coverage. Cieri's résumé includes seven years of coaching on the high school level, with three years as a successful high school head coach, posting an 18-9 record. Cieri, who holds a master's in science education, attributes his passion for improving skills and techniques with a sharp eye on special teams organization to his 38 years of experience as an advanced placement biology teacher and science chairperson.